TAKE US
TO THE
TOP

*The 25 Steps to Leadership and
Organizational Success*

I0522135

GREGORY A. WARREN, Ed.D.

AMERICAN LAW ENFORCEMENT
TRAINING AND CONSULTING, LLC
American Law Enforcement Publishing
Warwick, MD

ISBN 979-8-9888320-0-3

Design and publishing assistance by The Happy Self-Publisher.

Dedicated to my family, who without their help, encouragement, and patience, this work could not have been completed. Susan, Hunter, Carey, Spenser, Sarah, Ellison, Reagan, McKenna and Parker

INTRODUCTION

E ven after working in many different types of organizations over the last 40 years, I still have not met anyone who did not want to be happy, fulfilled and successful both personally and professionally! How is it then that so many people today are unhappy, unfulfilled and dissatisfied with where they work or what they do while they are at work? There has to be a key to unlocking the hidden potential of every American who struggles every day to excel in their chosen profession and organization! Whether you are a team member just starting out, or already holding a major leadership position within the organization, there are several major keys to unlocking both you and the organization's potential for high performance and success! Every American today deserves the opportunity to try to find out how to unleash their potential for both high performance and happiness. Our world of work here in the Unites States is changing rapidly as are the expectations of our employee workforce. We as team members and our organizations have to learn how to foster and grow both personal happiness and professional high performance if we expect to be successful today! This is the purpose and thrust behind *Take Us to the Top: The 25 Steps to Leadership and Organizational Success!* We can identify at least 25 critical steps to leadership, high performance and organizational success! The following 25 chapters will provide you with the critical steps and keys to reaching your full potential as a team member or leader within your organization! Prepare to learn how each chapter in *Take Us to the Top: The 25 Steps to Leadership and Organizational Success,* unlocks yet another of the 25 secrets to attaining high performance as an individual and success as an organization!

TABLE OF CONTENTS

You can't be a high-performance organization today without great leadership and a great employee workforce. Great leaders and team members will instill high performance in others and ignite the enthusiasm required of high performance and a great organization!

Identify your vision and set the direction of the organization for it via a well-designed and innovative strategic plan, designed purposely to accomplish the organization's mission and vision in an exemplary manner.

Design and develop a comprehensive strategic plan and ensure you don't skip any parts or steps.

Communicate your team's and organization's goals, objectives and priorities to all team members and stakeholders.

How you develop the organization's strategic plan and the "buy in" you gain by including everyone in the process, is just as critical to success as the plan itself. Ensure you involve all team members in the plan's development if you want to gain a "shared vision".

Ensure you structure the organization appropriately, and also secure all of the resources needed for plan implementation and mission accomplishment.

Build high performance teams by leveraging your organization's various types and levels of diversity, and creativity.

Engage in effective human resources and talent management practices including recruiting, selecting, onboarding, training, developing, and promoting the very best talent available!

Plan thoroughly and prepare for the effective implementation of the plan and remember to successfully manage the change required for success.

Utilize proven Organizational Management principles and standardized business practices to maximize efficiency and effectiveness throughout your team and the organization.

Make sure you don't jump to conclusions too quickly and always make sure your decisions make sense if you expect others to have confidence in you and follow you.

Communicate continually where the organization has been, where it is currently, and where it is going in the future! People are starved for information and want to know; remember they have a very vested interest in what is going on internally and how it affects them personally and professionally!

Model the expected behavior and standards of performance. Lead the way by showing everyone how to always remain professional in any situation!

To increase your situational performance, strive to learn about yourself, both your strengths and weaknesses, and ask what qualities or concerns others see and recognize in you, that you cannot?

Develop successful work designs and workflows, and minimize team member frustration by ensuring the organization's systems and processes again are functioning correctly!

Identify individual, team and corporate values, enforce ethical standards, and identify and limit risk to help build a strong and viable organization.

Ensure your individual, team and organizational values and work performance standards support a positive work environment and organizational culture.

Remember your Core Competencies, Signature Strengths and Competitive Advantages, and build and sustain both short term and long-term relationships that support them.

Engage in effective succession planning to ensure the organization's future viability, by identifying and developing your organization's current and future talent! People want a chance to learn, grow and develop themselves both personally and professionally!

PREFACE

Take us to the Top: The 25 Steps to Leadership and Organizational Success, was born out of the need to provide both students and practitioners of leadership, organizational management, and human performance, with a pragmatic approach to becoming a high performance and successful organization today. This work helps prepare all of us who are interested in achieving high performance and success today, to do our jobs more efficiently and effectively, without having to experience the negative by-products of constantly experimenting with various leadership styles, perspectives and approaches depending upon the situation faced. There are educators who state, "Let's try it; all we can do is fail." This statement is a testament to those who play the game without any real stakes or consequences. For everyone else who works in the real world, needs their job, and cares about their career and the organization they have given so much to, failure is the proverbial "not an option." The negative impact experienced with failure can be devastating to the individual, the team, and even the entire organization! *Take Us to the Top: The 25 Steps to Leadership and Organizational Success* is designed to show you how to not only survive as a team member or leader today, but how to thrive and succeed as an organization as well!

SECTION 1

Leading Success

CHAPTER 1

FOSTER GREAT LEADERSHIP TO DRIVE ORGANZIATIONAL SUCCESS!

You can't be a high-performance organization today without great leadership and a great employee workforce. Great leaders, team members and organizations help ignite the enthusiasm required of high performance at every level!

S ome die young, some are killed, and some even cut their own throat, so to speak but only a few live a long, successful, and prosperous life. I am not talking about people. I am talking about organizations: for-profit businesses and industries, non-profits both large and small, those from the field of education, and even local, state, and federal government entities. For as much as society has progressed in the 21st century, we must still find a way for all of these diverse organizations to successfully meet the many challenges they face, both internally and externally. From competition to major advances in technology, to trying to find both qualified and highly motivated workers, organizations today both big and small all face similar challenges. Sure, the names might change, and some are littered with acronyms only the military could appreciate, but in the end, we all as members of various types of organizations, hope to work somewhere that has a truly meaningful mission and vision, and which stands for something bigger than just ourselves or money. We want to work somewhere that makes us feel special and satisfies our innate human desire for belonging, personal development, and professional growth.

Anyone who has tried can see that finding the secret to operating a successful organization is not an easy task. Many times, as organizations become larger and more successful, they simultaneously become more complex. They become more challenging for leadership to direct and control. Maintaining focus and effectively motivating the employee workforce under these conditions becomes the new daily challenge, regardless of the number of variables present. Keeping one's eye on the prize and aiming for the organization's target goals and objectives is not as simple as many might think. Anyone involved in the game of trying to operate an organization in an effective and successful manner can relate to what I'm saying. No one knows until they have had the yoke and weight of such responsibility resting on their shoulders, what the pressures, stressors, and frustrations are that come with the duties and activities of leading an organization.

The various administrative, operational, and supports services responsibilities and demands in any large organization are many, including the ability to change when required.

There are many documented cases of organizations failing to make the necessary changes required to survive. Sometimes the challenges are more than the organization's leadership can predict, prevent, recognize, or adjust to in a timely manner. A perfect example of this is how only 45 of the original Fortune 500 companies first identified in the 1950s still hold the honor of being listed among the Fortune 500 today. A quick study reveals why this phenomenon has occurred. Yes, changes in world markets, increased competition from abroad, changes in societal values, etc., can all negatively impact how strong a company is and whether they can sustain themselves as a high performing organization for the long haul. However, when one starts to really study why many of these companies fell off the Fortune 500 list, one can readily see many of the problems started, or were at least exacerbated from within, such as: possessing a mission which was no longer relevant to the customer or the world's needs, changes in employee workforce demographics, possessing or embracing ineffective processes and systems, being outpaced by new technologies, and most of all complacency among leaders who "were asleep at the wheel." Inept leaders providing at best poor or even non-existent leadership. For these reasons, many corporations have fallen from grace in recent decades. Similarly, some governmental entities across the country have also been dissolved, privatized, merged, or renamed, all in an effort to make them either more efficient or effective. For example, many local police departments today have joined with other county or municipal police operations to become what are commonly referred to as metro departments and regional police departments. Another example of a complacent organization would be the Defense Protective Service (DPS) which was quickly alleviated of its responsibilities and duty to protect the United States Pentagon shortly after the 9/11 attack. The Pentagon is now protected by a new organization, the Pentagon Force Protection Agency. The list goes on and on, but the point is that whether you are a for-profit, non-profit, education, or government entity, you can be made to "go away" today if you are not accomplishing your mission in an exemplary manner!

Many organizations suffering from the serious issues and concerns mentioned above will surely fall even farther, possibly reaching a full-blown downward spiral or collapse. This occurs at an even greater pace and to a higher degree when the system and its many players are placed under increasing degrees of stress from poor or ineffective leadership. Like the stress placed on a chain while pulling a heavy load, the weakest links break first. Organizations are not unlike a chain. Each individual team member, team, or function within the organization comprises the individual links of the chain. There are even times when one link breaking can immediately cause others to do likewise, due to the pervasiveness, interrelatedness, and negative synergy of some of the problems that may abound throughout the organization. This is all exacerbated when the systems and processes required for large organizations to succeed fail to operate as prescribed or designed.

Because so many organizations have failed throughout history, we should all become ever more vigilant as to how we design, operate, and sustain our various institutions, businesses and organizations today. There is an assumption in the United States that leadership drives organizational success. I believe the following chapters will solidify this belief. Organizational success is measured by the ability to accomplish the organization's mission and vision in an exemplary fashion, and great leadership is required to drive both high performance and success at every level, from the individual members of the employee workforce to the entire organization as a whole!

SECTION 2

The Strategic Plan

CHAPTER 2

IDENTIFY A VISION AND SET YOUR DIRECTION FOR IT!

Identify your vision and set the direction of the organization towards it via the development of a strategic plan, designed solely and implemented purposely to accomplish the organization's identified mission and agreed upon vision.

E very organization, no matter how small, large, simple, or complex, must have a "reason for being." In other words, why do they exist? There must be a reason why the governing entity to which the organization reports, would spend the time, money, and energy required to "stand up" a new, or maintain an existing entity. It is very hard to justify the design, development, and growth of an organization which does not have a necessary reason for being. How will the leadership for the organization set direction, identify goals, and gain the commitment of team members without a well-defined mission? A mission must be clearly articulated to everyone, explaining clearly why the organization exists and is important.

Once the organization's mission has been established, top leadership must agree to it, and accept the responsibility to accomplish the identified and agreed upon mission. The real questions for both the governing body and top leadership of the organization are, "How well do we want to accomplish the mission?", and "what direction does the organization need to head, in order to accomplish the mission in an exemplary manner?" The answers to these two questions typically comprise the vision of the organization.

In order for all of this to be realized, the governing body for the organization must ensure the mission is legitimate and validate the organization's very existence, designating it as both a necessity and priority. Identifying an organization, or at least its mission as a priority is a minimum requirement for any type of lofty or challenging vision to be realized. If the mission is not a priority, then more times than not, the much-needed leadership, personnel, equipment, time, money, technology, and other necessary resources required for success, will not be made available or leveraged to the greatest possible effect for the organization. Therefore, we must always remember to identify and understand the mission for which we have signed on for and determine whether it is indeed a priority. Then we can set the direction for the organization, with an agreed upon mission and "shared vision", where all members of the organization have solidified their personal and professional commitment to achieving it in an exemplary manner. As Kouzes and Posner discuss in their book *The Leadership Challenge*, all members of the employee workforce possessing a "shared vision" is critical to leadership effectiveness and organizational success. Success is all about setting direction for the organization in accordance with one's designated organizational mission and agreed upon, "shared vision".

Picking the right leader with the vision to set a good direction and drive the strategic planning process towards that vision is paramount. With this end in mind, strong corporate or political jurisdictional governance should endeavor to find a leader who possesses all of the many competencies and qualities the organization needs to achieve success. There are many personality traits and general characteristics that organizations typically look for in their top leaders and chief executive officers. Two of the most obvious examples, are in the words of the late General Norman Schwarzkopf: "character" and "competence." General Schwarzkopf, the supreme allied commander for Operation Desert Storm in the 1990 Iraqi War, stated more than once, that great leaders need to have the competence and the ability to achieve the results that their appointing and or governing body expects, as well as the character, political will, and tenacity to see it through to the end. Ability, whether it is intellectual in nature, or some type of technical skill set, is great in and of itself, but if you don't have the drive, the stamina, and the ethical character to see your mission through to fruition, then what good will come from all of your efforts? I have seen this phenomenon occur many times in a wide variety of organizations, both large and small, where top leadership possessed one or the other of these two qualities, but not both. There were times when the balance required to achieve true effectiveness within the organization was absent, and so the success that was expected failed to materialize. Jim Collins, in his 2001 bestseller *Good to Great*, espouses the same premise. Jim Collins and his research team revealed that out of all of the successful organizations that they studied over a multi-year period, two leadership characteristics almost always rang true. The effective leaders possessed a great degree of humility, and yet were extremely tenacious in their desire to achieve the results expected of both themselves, and the organization. One might initially believe that these two qualities openly contradict one another. That is not necessarily true. I agree wholeheartedly with Jim Collins, that without humility, leaders (particularly those at higher levels) begin believing that they have all of the answers. I believe the higher you go in the organization many times, the more your own self-worth and ability can become artificially inflated, leaving you to believe that you truly do have all of the answers.

One past example of this phenomenon was the flagrant rift between President Truman, Congress, and General Douglas MacArthur, who was the supreme allied commander of Allied forces during the

Korean Conflict. General MacArthur failed to follow the desires and direction of both the United States Congress, and President Truman. Instead, he intentionally worked towards proving his own points and furthering his own personal agenda by continuing to antagonize the Chinese during the conflict. MacArthur continued to antagonize the Chinese, even though he was warned not to continue engaging in such dangerous tactics and maneuvers so close to the Chinese border. President Truman was so concerned, as were members of Congress, that he ordered General MacArthur to return to the U.S. to discuss his actions in Korea. The General responded to the President's order by stating that he was too busy to meet. President Truman then agreed to meet MacArthur halfway, on the tiny Pacific Island of Guam. Again, General MacArthur proved his contempt for political leadership by showing various signs of disrespect to the President. General MacArthur placated Truman by promising not to push the Chinese any further, but even after his meeting with, and warning by the President not to continue escalating the situation in Korea, General MacArthur went back to having his forces engage in various tactics that would continue to heighten the concerns of the Chinese. Finally, the Chinese invaded North Korea with over 400,000 troops, killing, wounding, and capturing thousands of Allied troops, and causing the Allied forces to hastily retreat. Macarthur's response to all of this was to ask President Truman to authorize the use of nuclear weapons against China. This is a blatant example of why picking the right leader who understands your mission and shares in your vision for the organization is critical to success! Governing bodies cannot afford to put the wrong person in charge of an organization. The costs of doing this can be devastating to the organization and its members in many different ways.

Therefore, all great leaders should actively engage in collecting data, gathering information, and using business intelligence, including scanning, analyzing, forecasting, predicting trends, and identifying patterns of behavior, etc., as they make critical decisions affecting the future of the organization and its success. I would like to believe that few, if any, governing boards or CEOs hope to simply achieve the status quo while in power. Poor performance, or failure, is normally not an option for many. That is not to say that there have not been times when an organization has been sold, merged with, or taken over due to its poor performance. For those public-sector entities and organizations that can be identified as no longer relevant, they can easily have their funding cut or charter revoked, due to their lackluster performance. As far as for-profit examples, there are too many to list them all. As mentioned earlier, of the original Fortune 500 companies that existed in 1954, the first year the list was published, only 45 of those original companies still remain part of the Fortune 500. That means that the other 455 companies have either been so successful that some other larger company wanted to purchase them, or the company's performance was less than desired or expected and they were dissolved or absorbed in some manner or fashion. This could mean the sale of the business, acquisition by another company, hostile takeover or outright declaration of bankruptcy by the organization. Because of the stakes in operating these large organizations being so high, regardless of their mission to make money, provide a service, or to serve a special interest in the non-profit arena, setting direction and correctly identifying priorities is critical to both their current and future viability.

Every top leader must identify a vision for their organization. In short, the mission is the "why do we exist?" and the vision is the "how good do we want to be?", or "how well do we as an organization want to accomplish our mission?" Let's face it, Americans love a winner, and second place or worse is unacceptable. I have never heard of an Olympic team, or troop in battle, who hoped to come in second. One thing is for sure in this very competitive world that we both work and live in, and that is that if you don't want to be first, you will surely never be first! So, the question then becomes, how do we as members of an organization, and particularly those of us in leadership positions, set a vision and put our direction into play? Again, we must identify exactly where we want to be. The Gap Analysis is designed with the intention of helping leaders identify "where their organizations are now", versus "where they want their organization to be"? If we can quantify or qualify what the difference is between the two statuses, then we can identify what we need to concentrate our current and future efforts on if we ever hope to be successful. However, there is another very important step to consider before completing this effort. One of the worst things a leader can do is try to identify alone what should be done to achieve future success. Due to the many hidden agendas, system complexities, and skewed perspectives and perceptions we all hold, no one leader or even group of stakeholders should convince themselves that they alone understand all there is to know about a specific task or operation, and that they alone harbor all the wisdom that is needed to achieve the mission of the organization in an exemplary fashion. The SWOT Analysis is the key component to completing this phase of the strategic planning process successfully. This analysis requires several steps and should involve representatives of all organizational stakeholder groups in some way, shape or form. This input, as with all data collected, must be factual and accurate in nature if it is to be of any use. The raw data, once collected, compiled, and collated into a usable format, must be analyzed thoroughly in an effort to make it informative and useful for the organization. With more in-depth analysis, this information can many times become useful business intelligence, and help ensure that the leaders in critical decision-making positions will be capable of making informed, rational decisions, which assist the organization in preventing problems and crises in the future. If an unwanted crisis does arise, this information will help the organization respond to it in an appropriate manner, which should assist in keeping them competitive and viable in the future.

With all of this in mind and recognizing the importance of gathering accurate data and intelligence, we must use a variety of methods to amalgamate the data collected. The SWOT Analysis is designed to make this activity possible. One very critical key to obtaining accurate information during the SWOT analysis is to ensure that those involved are knowledgeable, credible, and honest in their observations and opinions regarding the various parts of the organization.

The SWOT analysis stands for and includes:

- Strengths – possessed by the organization.
- Weaknesses – to be aware of by the organization.
- Opportunities – available to the organization.
- Threats – faced either now or in the future by the organization.

The collection of this type of information is so very important to those in decision making positions, particularly when developing their vision, setting direction, identifying priorities, and aligning the organization's goals, objectives and even resources within their own internal and external operating environments. Evaluating and reporting on everything is critical. For example, from how the organization is communicating both internally and externally, to the external political environment that currently exist, those responsible for the organization's performance must have the right information and intelligence available to make the right decisions. Everyone from line level employees, to technicians, supervisors, managers, scientists, accountants, and even top leadership, should all be solicited for input as to where the organization currently stands and what it's obvious and not so obvious assets and liabilities are?

Several different methods that can be utilized to collect this large amount of data, information, and intelligence are included below.

Some of those methods and options are:

- Utilizing various, diverse focus groups.
- Surveying verbally, in writing, or electronically, a random sample of individuals from each of the stakeholder groups.
- Asking for white papers and feasibility studies to be completed.
- Contracting or outsourcing an organizational analysis.
- Reviewing annual reports, strategic plans, current budgets, and even past budgets.
- Reviewing past state of the organization addresses.

Some of the information that would be considered important to policy and decision makers would include the following:

- Media coverage (positive or negative)
- Morale of employees
- Dedication and commitment levels of various individuals, groups or teams
- Number of past and current internal grievances
- Lawsuits pending (internal and external)
- Budget and fiscal control issues
- Production, sales and inventory levels
- Past profit margins
- Organizational core competencies, signature strengths, and competitive advantage
- Physical resources and their condition
- Prevailing human resources management practices
- Current policies, procedures, and processes
- Use of current and future technologies
- Obtaining new, or loss of current certifications and accreditations

As one can see, this process produces not only a large amount of data, but also critical information and intelligence. If missing, it could cause a great many decisions to be made without the necessary research and contemplation required of a good decision. Many times, poor information results in poor decisions. There is no excuse for this when you are in the top leadership position of an organization, and so much rests on your vision and direction for the organization.

One last, but very important item to take into consideration when collecting data within an organization is to understand that some of the information may be tainted, skewed, or contaminated. I learned this firsthand early on in my consulting career when I recognized that a great many of the responses on the various SWOT Analyses, we were conducting were overly positive, even though things were typically bad enough that we were in fact being brought in to address many of the problems, issues, and concerns within the organization. It was at that time I decided to develop a second methodology for collecting the SWOT Analysis data, which would either corroborate or contradict the data and information in the original, overt type SWOT Analysis we had just conducted. I did this by waiting until we finished the formal, overt SWOT Analysis, and while everything was still fresh in everyone's minds and we still had undedicated time at our disposal, I would hand out a simple form called the Modified SWOT Analysis. This form asks for each respondent to anonymously list what problems, issues, or concerns they were currently facing in the organization and one recommendation or solution for each of the items they had just listed. These Modified SWOT Analyses were completed individually and turned in anonymously. It was enlightening to see the information contained on these forms, that had not been identified or recorded during the original, open SWOT Analysis completed earlier. My suspicions were confirmed, that if supervisors were present, or if any employees were present and perceived as being "snitches", then many colleagues would fail to engage in the original SWOT Analysis discussions openly and honestly. We were not only losing engagement during the original SWOT Analysis, but the quality and validity of the input diminished when this negative presence was felt. We lost truthful feedback regarding what problems were being experienced and to what degree within the organization they were occurring. Since then, I have been using and prescribing to others a Modified SWOT Analysis before dismissing for the day or finishing up the regular SWOT Analysis activities, with very open, honest and candid results!

CHAPTER 3

HOW ARE WE GOING TO GET THERE? DEVELOPING THE STRATEGIC PLAN!

Build a comprehensive strategic plan and ensure you don't skip any parts or steps.

Leadership is indeed an integral part to driving high performance. Leaders make decisions to either act or not to act, all in an effort to ensure everyone executes the various tasks identified in the strategic plan appropriately. Accomplishing your mission and vision in an exemplary manner requires high performance at every level of the organization, from individual employees, to teams, to entire business divisions. Every individual member of the organization must engage in behavior which adds value to the organization. That means executing each and every task required of them per the organization's strategic plan and the items specified in their own individual annual performance appraisal's goals and objectives section.

Steps to developing an effective strategic plan:

- Understand and accept the organization's mission!
- Assess the organization's assets, liabilities, and overall readiness!

- Identify a realistic, yet challenging vision!
- Set direction and identify priorities!
- Identify and articulate general goals!
- Develop correlating performance objectives for each goal!
- Prepare appropriate strategies for the accomplishment of each objective!
- Plan, prepare, and gather the necessary or requisite resources!
- Design and develop each of the processes and systems required for functionality to occur!
- Implement, plan, and execute all tasks via supervisors embedding of the organization's goals and objectives into each employee's annual performance appraisal!
- Assess progress regularly and at all levels (ongoing process, not an isolated point in time)!
- Modify the plan as needed to further enhance or sustain desired performance levels!

As one can see, the strategic planning process itself is really not that difficult to understand; however, it is sequential in nature and therefore must be tackled with due diligence and the "managing of the process" it deserves. It must also ascertain accurate and timely input from all affected stakeholders, to help ensure it has adequate access to the business intelligence it requires, and of course the necessary "buy in" needed to ensure success. Unfortunately, in the United States, there is more of a need now than ever before to work smarter, not harder. Organizations must deal with the scarce resources and budgetary restrictions that exist, and all while responding to other independent variables such as economic trends, competition, and even pandemics and other unexpected national emergencies. Hence the need for a well-developed strategic plan, with very well-defined goals and objectives, which are realistic yet challenging in nature, involving everyone in the organization working together towards the agreed upon mission, and identified "shared vision"!

Some helpful tips to developing an effective strategic plan can be found in the following:

- Keep it simple!
- Seek input and buy-in from all stakeholders!
- Keep the goals and objectives challenging, yet realistic!
- Concentrate on your organization's core competencies!
- Don't over-saturate the organization and its members with too much change too quickly!
- Prioritize your efforts and concentrate on quality, not quantity!
- Assess progress regularly!

Remember, the entire reason for an organization's existence is the successful accomplishment of the agreed upon mission and attainment of the identified vision. The real problem exists many times in convincing organizational stakeholders that a comprehensive strategic plan is really critical to the organization's current and future viability. Once convinced of the need for positive, proactive change and the fact that the strategic plan is how the organization will make those changes become a reality, we must train and educate all team members and stakeholders of the organization as to what a strategic plan is and how it really works. People can't implement and execute what they don't understand. It is evident that most internal organizational stakeholders, including many of those in leadership positions today, don't even understand the basic nomenclature of a strategic plan, much less how to effectively develop and implement one through the use of various effective strategic planning and strategic management processes.

The basic parts and steps to a typical strategic plan:

Mission – Accept the mission and engage in both a SWOT and Gap analyses.

Vision - Develop a "shared vision."

Goals – Set direction through general goals and identifying specific priorities.

Objectives – Design (SMART – Specific, Measurable, Attainable, Realistic & Timely) objectives and ask for input from the field for developing both Objectives and Strategies.

Strategies – Identify and develop the "how" do we accomplish the above objectives.

Work Plans – Embed (Action plans into each employee's annual performance appraisal under their own personal and professional goals and objectives section).

It is also critically important to the strategic plan's success to ensure you have a mechanism in place to monitor progress and implement change when and where necessary. As one can see, developing a strategic plan requires organization and coordination, with each part being designed and developed sequentially, otherwise what you try to implement will ultimately fail. So, in short, it isn't simply having a plan, it is how you developed the plan that is just as important. I can assure you, how you develop your organization's strategic plan is critical to the organization's current and future success!

CHAPTER 4

IDENTIFY YOUR PERFORMANCE OBJECTIVES AND MAJOR PRIORITIES!

Communicate both your team's and organization's goals, objectives and priorities to all team members and stakeholders.

The size and complexity of most organizations today, coupled with the limited resources many times available, allows for only so many priorities to be addressed at any one time. If your organization is for-profit in nature, the owners or stockholders expect over-head to remain low and profit margins to remain steady or high. The return on profit to either the owner or shareholders is paramount and the primary reason for your existence. If you are operating in an educational, military, governmental, or non-profit environment, then your political jurisdiction's governing body, such as a board of trustees, board of directors, or legislative body, will expect you to use taxpayers', and or donator's dollars as efficiently and effectively as possible. As a leader, one must be mindful of this expectation, so that the limited dollars available to the organization go as far as possible towards the accomplishment of the stated mission. With this end in mind, every leader must be cognizant of exactly what activities and efforts are priorities, so that they might correctly direct the commensurate type and level of resources required for the accomplishment of the organization's goals and objectives as identified in the strategic plan. One should always remember, "If everything is a priority, then nothing is a priority." There are only so many resources to go around, particularly in governmental based operations, where there are always tasks that must be accomplished, simply because there is no one else left to take care of them. Many times, in government-based operations, there are tasks that are simply considered "necessary evils". These tasks unfortunately are many times not associated with being critical to the accomplishment of the goals and objectives in the strategic plan, or even the accomplishment of the mission itself, but nevertheless must still be addressed. There are also goals and objectives which are not completed very often and are low risk and low frequency, but for which you must still be prepared to address in case an occurrence or need does arise. Emergency planning within a governmental entity for instance, is not something that elected officials enjoy spending large amounts of money on. Just like purchasing insurance on a personal basis, no one wants to spend money on something they hope will never have to be used. An organization, however, must be prepared for that rare event or occurrence. Many professional planners today, like many project managers state, "hope for the best, and plan for the worst".

In a for-profit arena, a corporation may not necessarily want to support certain community-based programs, yet leadership within the organization recognizes the role they must play as part of their public relations programming. In fact, in some states like Delaware for instance, the Community Reinvestment Act mandates that financial institutions that want to base their operations within Delaware's corporate friendly environment, expend specific amounts of money on various philanthropic endeavors that assist the community in general. The funds expended on these types of activities don't necessarily or directly impact the organization's bottom line, yet must be considered important and be met, as it is many times the proverbial "cost of doing business."

These examples and many more show how priorities must be identified so that the proper amount of planning and resourcing can be completed in order to both prepare for and execute the tasks associated with accomplishing the goals and objectives identified as major priorities in the organization's strategic plan. Members of the organization should remember that every leadership team has "pet projects", or priorities, which many times equate to organizational priorities; therefore, every employee should be prepared to work as efficiently as possible so that the limited funds, technology, human resources, and other tangible resources available, can be directed to the areas where the "biggest bang for your buck" can be realized! Always remember to identify and adopt goals, objectives and priorities which are important to your organization's true and long-lasting success!

CHAPTER 5

INCLUDE EVERYONE IN THE STRATEGIC PLANNING PROCESS!

How you develop the organization's strategic plan and the "buy in" you gain by including everyone, is just as critical to success as the plan itself. Ensure you include all team members in the process if you want to gain a "shared vision"!

As with many things in life, it is not always where you end up, but how you get there that counts. The age-old adage "it isn't always about the destination, but the journey" that counts, also holds true with strategic planning. The end doesn't always justify the means, particularly when dealing with people. The strategic plan is so critical to the current and future viability of an organization that it is hard to fathom highly performing organizations not having one. In the end, even the best and most advanced strategic plans will fail if they are not 1) correct or the right plan with the right goals, objectives, and strategies for achieving the organization's mission and vision in an exemplary manner, and 2) being supported by all personnel regardless of rank, position, or tenure within the organization. If those responsible for the accomplishment of the many and varied tasks required for the successful implementation of the strategic plan do not support it, then it will inevitably fail. This failure stems from a lack of commitment which in turn will be realized by a lack of effort and motivation to perform the required tasks.

One of the basic tenets of human performance is motivation. Employees are not typically motivated to perform tasks voluntarily if they do not understand how valuable completing those tasks are, or if they do not agree with the strategies and methods identified for completing them. The only way to address these two critical factors is to engage the employee workforce both personally and professionally, during every step of the strategic planning process. No one knows how to get things done better in an organization than those who are closest to the "front line." While the organization's governing body and top leadership may set direction, how tasks actually get done in the organization is many times best left up to those who are closest to the task at hand, and their direct supervisors. By involving everyone in the strategic planning process, you gain more factual, realistic, and insightful information, which of course ultimately leads to better business intelligence with which to make both better business and operational decisions. Involving the employee workforce in the strategic planning process also reveals your degree of respect for your personnel and their ability, while also providing them with a sense of personal worth and professional growth. In short, they realize that you respect them and trust them, and they believe that what they say and do counts. The worth of this very positive by-product of the strategic planning process is immeasurable.

You cannot direct and/or order the implementation of a strategic plan and just expect it to occur. The daily implementation of the strategic plan entails large numbers of people attempting to complete incredibly large numbers of individual tasks during every minute of the day, sometimes throughout every day of the year. Even with high levels of accountability and supervision, employees and team members must remain continually motivated to successfully implement the goals and objectives contained within the organization's strategic plan. You must have "buy-in," for success in any endeavor, and one of the most successful methods to garner "buy-in" is through soliciting input. The failure of leadership to engage both employees and all other stakeholders from throughout the organization in the strategic planning process will undoubtedly cost them dearly in the future.

Sometimes the most obvious and basic steps to a process hold the answer to successfully completing more complex and complicated processes within the organization. The basic steps to strategic plan development and implementation must be completed thoroughly, inclusively, and sequentially, if the organization is expected to continue to be successful. Therefore, we must never forget the criticality of including everyone in the strategic planning process if we ever hope to be a great organization! Asking team members from every rank and seniority level from throughout the organization to participate in both the SWOT and Gap analyses would be a great start. However, asking the same group to provide input into developing future performance objectives also provides critical stakeholders with another voice in solidifying the organization's future. Lastly, what better way to conclude than by asking for input from team members and asking them for ideas as to how to best achieve those same objectives just identified for inclusion in the new strategic plan. Asking team members and other stakeholders what strategies should be used to accomplish the organization's upcoming/future objectives is an excellent way to both garner accurate and timely information and business intelligence, while simultaneously continuing to build the respect and trust of team members and the entire employee workforce. Again, I cannot emphasize enough the "buy-in" that will be realized by the organization by asking the employee workforce what strategies should be developed and utilized to accomplish the various objectives as set forth in the strategic plan. Remember, the increased loyalty to both the organization and the organization's leadership, and hence commitment to the mission in general, by including everyone in the strategic planning process, cannot be overstated!

SECTION 3

Structuring the Organization and Resourcing the Plan

CHAPTER 6

BUILD THE ORGANZIATIONAL STRUCTURE AND RESOURCE THE PLAN!

Ensure you structure the organization appropriately, and also secure all of the resources needed for plan implementation and mission accomplishment.

E very organization has a structure. Some are meticulously planned, designed, and built to fulfill very specific organizational needs, and others may even be thought of as revolutionary. Others just seem to have come together over time or by happenstance. These would be considered more evolutionary in nature. I think we are safe in saying that from ancient times and the first formalized communities in Mesopotamia, to the Romans perfecting and formalizing the very regimented design of their military legions, we can recognize that the larger your organization is and the more critical your mission is, the more important your organizational structure and organizational management practices become to your future success and viability.

Structure isn't designed to be punitive in nature as many people believe; however, it is necessary to direct and control all of the many individual efforts, tasks and resources required for the accomplishment of the organization's strategic plan. The United States military is another example of a very regimented, hierarchical designed entity, which must by its very nature, size, and mission possess a very formal and well-delineated structure. The number of policies, directives, procedures, and processes required to effectively accomplish the missions of such large organizations is innumerable and requires well-designed, comprehensive workflows and work design structures. The structure of an organization can be based upon many different variables, such as mission, geography, functionality, tradition, and even past successes and failures. There is no way to direct everyone's efforts, much less realize their potential synergy, if not for the use of effective structures and organizational control systems.

You must first identify what specific entities, functions and processes are desired, or required, in order to effectively implement the many goals, objectives, and strategies in a typical organizational strategic plan. Most of the entities or business divisions identified below, not only possess the authority, but also retain the responsibility for the functions and processes typically found within the confines of any large or complex entity. See Integrated Strategic Management Systems, or ISMS, in Chapter 11 for further details.

The following are some examples of the more readily accepted organizational functions required of most standardized business, non-profit, and governmental operations:

- Executive Offices
- Budget and Fiscal Control
- Research and Development
- Legal Counsel
- Supply Chain and Purchasing
- Logistics

- Security
- Human Resources Management
- Information Technology
- Marketing
- Public Relations
- Production
- Facilities and Maintenance
- Sales
- Compliance or Inspections (accreditation)

The next step in implementing the organization's strategic plan is to identify, locate, and ascertain the funding, talent, time, materials, equipment/supplies, and technology required of each individual task identified in the strategic plan. Most people agree that today's work environment is extremely challenging and risk-filled, full of frustrations and potential liabilities. There is no faster way to solidify your employees' frustration levels with internal operations and decision making, than to not provide them with the necessary resources such as funding, time, materials, equipment, and supplies to do their jobs correctly. There is an old saying, "I have done so much, for so long, with so little, that I can do almost anything, with nothing." Now, if this were really true, it would be a great day for all employees, and their organizations, but the truth is that this type of adage spells out just how frustrated many workers have become with their organizations, particularly when they are so often expected to accomplish so much with so little. Granted, the lack of pleasing aesthetics in the building you work in, the antiquated tools you use, or even poor ergonomics in your work processes may not cause bankruptcy for your organization, but one or more of these in combination with other variables can surely affect your individual motivation towards high performance and operational efficiency.

Whether you negatively impact employees who provide customer service, or workers in a factory operating an assembly line, you will certainly not be maximizing everyone's effectiveness if high levels of frustration set in for whatever reason. This will ultimately have a negative effect on the organization's productivity and service levels. Frustrated employees, equal unhappy employees. Normally this will equate to a decrease in overall productivity and quality control with increases in wastefulness and risks. These factors can drastically undermine many other worthwhile efforts and eventually spread to and permeate every level of the organization.

A lack of funding can also equate to high levels of frustration in the employee workforce. At the risk of sounding cynical, most organizations operate at a level commensurate with the level of funding they have available. Let's face it; "it takes money to make money", or to at least make an organization "go". From salary requirements, to purchasing raw materials and keeping your supply chain functioning smoothly, you can only execute the tasks mandated in your organization's strategic plan to the degree in which you can pay for all of the resources required. So, we must identify how we are going to fund each of the tasks required for the proper implementation of our strategic plan's various goals, objectives, and strategies if we ever hope to succeed as an organization.

The first function of this task is to identify each, and every movement required of your operation, along with the administrative and support functions required of these same operations. You must then identify the level of funding required for each and every one of those functions and movements. There are times when it is difficult to identify or predict the exact level of funding that will be required of a certain function in the future. In those cases, one can look back on historical data, and if that isn't available, try to forecast as a contingent what funding will be necessary to operate successfully. When completed, you should be able to develop a budget that will, at a minimum, be able to guide your initial expenditures. Almost all budgets, due to the very nature of their criticality to an organization's operational efficiency, require daily, continuous, if not real-time and instantaneous updating and monitoring. With this comes the ability to make adjustments when necessary to ensure the organization is operating at its maximum level of efficiency and effectiveness. Real time revenue versus expenditures accounting, is almost required for ensuring smooth operations and administration in today's complex organizations.

Just as important as identifying how much money you will need and how it will be appropriated is the ability to identify the reliability and or consistency of those funding sources. There are obviously varying types and sources of funding available today, most of which are predicated upon the type of organization you are. Another key to remember is not only are there varying sources of funding earmarked for specific types of expenditures and or activities, such as service charges for specific request in the private sector, to grants in aid from a legislative body for a specific need in the not-for-profit sector, but the forms in which those funds can be found are also varied. Examples include profits being carried over, current profit being realized, profit from sales of products, the sale of real property, endowments, grants, private collaterally backed loans, government loans, sale of surplus property, and the sale of government backed bonds. When accepting outside funding of any type, always do your homework and research. There are important facets to be aware of when receiving and spending various types of outside funds. First, restrictions placed within the loan or grant contract, including interest on loans and tax implications on your organization, can vary greatly depending upon the source, or the use of the funding. Donated funds of various types also carry many times restrictive clauses, helping to guide the recipient on the who, what, when, where and how of spending those funds. Always check to be sure you have not assumed too much.

Ascertaining appropriate funding levels is critical for the continued operations and administration of an organization. The same premise holds true for the Information Technology (IT), and Management Information Systems (MIS) functions within your organization. You cannot expect employees to perform highly if they have not been afforded the necessary equipment, training, and tools in both hardware and software to get the job done correctly. No one would argue how critical technology is to today's operational effectiveness. So why, then, are we still trying to purchase the cheapest hardware, easiest software, and bid on the most archaic pieces of technology, with improper or poorly spelled-out specifications. All of this is complicated further by purchasing IT or MIS equipment or services without the necessary training or maintenance packages suggested to go with them. Because of this, many workers today share one of these sentiments: "We just purchased new software, and all they gave us was a 15-minute explanation on how to use it," or, conversely, "We did not receive any real hands-on training at all". Meanwhile, the organizational leadership expects its employees to effectively wait on customers or respond to client needs in a timely and pleasing manner, using the new technology made available, without providing even the most basic education or training.

For those who find themselves working in the world of production, protecting an efficient and effective supply chain is paramount. Without raw materials, components, parts, or usable data, an organization cannot possibly keep production at the desired levels. Even more than just having the materials or components coming in on time, there are less apparent items to take into consideration, such as the sequencing and/or quality of the items needed. Producing a quality product on time requires an effective operations management system, full of efficient and well-scheduled workflows. When materials arrive late, in the wrong order, or in an unusable or undesirable condition, the supply chain breaks down rapidly, causing a whole host of negative ripple effects that can unfortunately be felt throughout an organization. This is why I caution people, when using outside suppliers, to really gauge their ability to deliver to the specifications, standards, and minimum levels of performance you expect or will tolerate. Furthermore, one must identify possible alternatives or contingency plans should something go seriously wrong, particularly if some function or process is of a critical nature to one of your basic operations and or core competencies. Contingency plans can help minimize and alleviate the negative impact of these issues with suppliers or outside stakeholders should they occur. The best plan is not to wonder "if they will occur" but be prepared for "when they occur".

One need only look at the Boeing Corporation as they proceeded with the design, development, and manufacture of the 787, to recognize that outsourcing too much, too quickly, can result in catastrophic problems. Over 70% of the new Boeing 787 was outsourced to a myriad of companies, including those from Great Britain, France, Japan, Italy, and Korea. When an organization such as Boeing relies too heavily on others for its own performance, there are inherent risks which the organization must absorb. With such massive, complex and time sensitive production schedules at stake and on an international scale, and with such complicated components as airplane parts, one can only imagine how convoluted this process became. That is exactly what happened. Even some of Boeing's own engineers warned management that this would likely occur with such a large degree of outsourcing, but the warnings were ignored and Boeing become so entangled with work stoppages and late schedules, that they actually had to buy out some of the worst offending companies they had outsourced to, in order to simply take over direct control of the supply chain, and thus ensure their future work performance schedules would not be placed in further jeopardy. These are hard lessons to be learned for anyone, but if a large mega-company with Boeing's resources can make this mistake, then it can happen to any organization, and to you!

CHAPTER 7

LEVERAGE DIVERSITY AND BUILD THE RIGHT TEAM!

Develop your human resources and talent via leveraging your organization's diversity, and building effective, high-performance teams.

We have discussed in past chapters the need to keep the organization healthy and viable for the future. Of course, there are multiple ways of accomplishing this task, for example purchasing new equipment through an effective recapitalization program, obtaining the latest software available, designing your own software for specific purposes, or investing heavily in obtaining the talent base required to accomplish the many and varied tasks outlined in the organization's strategic plan. We should remember it is absolutely critical to organizational success to develop each employee individually and to provide them with opportunities to grow, and to expand their positive impact on the organization. Howard Schultz, of Starbucks, is a perfect example of reinvesting in all members of the organization, from entry-level employees to seasoned executives. By providing every employee, part-time or full-time, with medical benefits and profit-sharing options, Schultz solidified Starbucks' commitment to the employees and the organization's mission. The dividends this type of re-investment in employees makes cannot be overstated.

"Talent management and picking the right people for the right job," was a large part of Jim Collins' research for his 2001 book "Good to Great." In it, Collins revealed that one of the seven critical tenets or requirements of becoming a great organization was to not only recruit, select, and hire the right people, but to also ensure you place them in the right position within the organization – the "right seat on the bus" if you will. A great many employees today do not feel they have found the right organization to work in, but what is even more disturbing is that of those who are in the right organization, many feel they still have not been provided adequate opportunities to grow and develop to their fullest potential. The impact of such feelings of frustration and negligence are quite obvious in so many organizations today! Poor employee satisfaction results in poor morale, which results in poor motivation to perform highly, and thus negatively impacts the organization's productivity and future viability.

As a college professor, program chair, academic advisor, and college dean, I have had the opportunity to meet and speak with a wide variety of students from all walks of life, interests, and talent levels. In short, from military personnel and veterans, to government employees and educators, to non-profit leaders, and even retirees looking for a second career, an overwhelming majority of people feel dissatisfied, unhappy, disheartened, and/or completely disengaged at their current places of employment. The reasons for this vary greatly, but one of the more prevalent causes is poor leadership, coupled with an organization (via the leadership) that fails to recognize their employees' real area of expertise and worth. The employee is thus forced to continue to work in an arena where they feel less than satisfied, productive or fulfilled.

You don't have to study the science of human performance and its relationship to motivation very long to understand that satisfied, fulfilled, and happy employees almost always outperform those who are not. When we look at productivity, service levels, quality control, waste, and risk mitigation as your primary organizational indicators of performance, you can see that in every one of these critical areas of performance, a happy, motivated employee will always outperform other team members. If you have enough of these high performing individuals on board, you will ultimately have high performing teams, and thus a high performing organization! Therefore, even if it isn't convenient or politically expedient, I beg all of those powers-to-be in various leadership positions, and even those in ranking HR positions, to work their hardest at identifying and aligning the talents of their personnel, in the hope that they will, in turn, help their organizations successfully accomplish their missions and visions. Leadership must recognize that individual team members truly are the backbone of the organization!

With this same end in mind, we should all concentrate more effort on group dynamics, team building, and leveraging diversity within the organization. We should always try to identify better ways to harness the power of diversity and bring out the synergy that can be found when effective teams are created! Although we often fool ourselves into thinking they are, groups are not necessarily teams. Teams exhibit very specific characteristics. Learning how to take a group of individuals and build (Forming, Norming, Storming, and Conforming) a high performing team is of course critical to organizational success. It will be very challenging, if not impossible, to achieve the organization's mission if individual employees cannot put their own personal desires aside for the betterment of the organization and the agreed upon "shared vision". Leveraging your organization's diversity is so critical to success today. An extensive list of team characteristics is presented below and provides each of us with a better grasp of what real teams truly require and what we should be doing to accentuate the use of them when possible.

Characteristics of true and effective teams:

- Specific, well-defined roles for every member.
- Mutual respect and trust in one another.
- Sacrifice expected and accepted for the good of the team and the mission.
- Well established and agreed upon skills, knowledge and abilities.
- Well defined Work Performance Standards.
- Effective internal communications and conflict management.
- Well defined and competent leaders in place.

Unfortunately, diversity is often-times an overlooked source of synergy and team effectiveness, and even too many insecure and archaic leaders is viewed as a detriment. Diversity, however in the workplace, can provide an organization with enhanced viewpoints on creativity, innovation, problem solving and can many times offer fresh perspectives on how to accomplish the many tasks outlined in the organization's strategic plan. Yes, of course, diversity exists today in race, culture, and even religion, but when we discuss diversity in 21st century high performance organizations, we should also recognize that diversity includes, educational levels, geography, skills, knowledge, abilities, demographics, and even age! Truly great leaders will learn to relate to each of their team members and understand what each member brings to the table in terms of not just skill sets, but also in regard to values, personality traits, and even character. Then and only then can they really harness all of the talent that they have on board within their respective teams, thus assisting every individual team member in the organization in becoming a high-performing employee, who desires to accomplish the organization's mission and vision in an exemplary fashion!

CHAPTER 8

MANAGE YOUR ORGANIZATION'S TALENT FOR HIGH PERFORMANCE!

Engage in effective human resources and talent management practices including recruiting, selecting, onboarding, training, developing, and promoting the very best talent available!

The importance of effective human resources management to an organization's success cannot be overstated. Unfortunately for many years the "Personnel Section", was in many organizations a place where soon-to-be retired individuals, or individuals who were not capable of effectively managing true operational responsibilities within the organization, would find themselves assigned. In the last couple of decades, a variety of new state and federal laws, coupled with litigation resulting from poor personnel decisions, has caused even the most steadfast opponents of strong human resources management functions, to recognize just how critical the many facets of effective human resources management are to an organization's current and future viability. Before studying any of the specific functions comprising any comprehensive, full-service HR department, we must first identify exactly what responsibilities and duties exist in an HR department today.

Below you will see a sampling of some of the more obvious and critical elements comprising a modern, full-service HR department in any typical, large organization today.

- Conducting a job task analysis or assembling a mission essential tasks list
- Developing commensurate job descriptions
- Recruiting necessary talent
- Conducting the personnel selection process
- Conducting a thorough orientation and onboarding process
- Conducting necessary training
- Managing the OJT and probationary process
- Managing the annual performance appraisal process
- Developing all required in-service, elective, and advanced training programs
- Administering the promotional process
- Processing all requests for transfers and job assignment positions
- Administering the drug testing program
- Investigating all HR complaints for protected classes of employees
- Conducting federally mandated training on ADA, sexual harassment, FLSA, FMLA, etc.
- Conducting and managing the organization's progressive discipline program
- Managing any remedial training that has been identified via disciplinary action.
- Conducting all collective bargaining negotiations
- Administering the payroll system

- Administering all employee benefit programs, including health insurance
- Administering all federally mandated diversity and EEOC activities
- Collecting and archiving all human resources related business records
- Preparing employees for retirement
- Conducting exit interviews

The above represents a variety of very important and challenging HR functions that must be conducted in a moral, ethical and legal manner today. Any mistakes made in this area can easily result in a complaint to a state or the Federal Department of Labor, or even end up in state or federal court for litigation.

The first, but many times overlooked function of effective human resource management is the conducting of a Job Tasks Analysis (JTA) in order to prepare a comprehensive Mission Essential Tasks List or (METL). This is truly the first step in preparing accurate job descriptions for the organization's various jobs and positions. This assists the organization in deciding which positions should be filled by employees internally, recruited externally, or which should be outsourced or contracted to those who already possess specific skills, knowledge and abilities. Some positions may even possibly be filled by temps and/or casual seasonal employees, volunteers, or even interns whenever possible. None of these decisions can be made by leadership without having first identified the specific requirements of each job position and classification. There are a variety of ways to complete this task and a number of groups that can conduct it on behalf of the organization. Some state and large local governmental departments of labor can complete a JTA, as well as private consultants. Many colleges and universities also have the ability to complete a JTA or METL. There are even HR firms and national professional groups who have completed generic Job Tasks Analyses for many of the more popular jobs and positions prevalent in our work force today. These can be easily purchased and utilized as a starting point for this very important and critical task.

Some of the more popular methods of completing a comprehensive Job Tasks Analysis are as follows:

- Candid observation and documentation of the various tasks, skills, and aptitudes of the job in question.
- Interviewing those who currently complete the tasks associated with the position in question.
- Completion of surveys by those who interact with this position and its various responsibilities.
- Interviewing the supervisors and managers who interact with the position.
- Reviewing video of those currently accomplishing the tasks of the position in question.
- Focus group discussions involving the position and its various requirements, duties and responsibilities.

Any number of these options can be effective, but it is always advisable to triangulate this process, similar to conducting any other type of research. Never accept the results of just one source of data. It is best to conduct at least three types of separate research and data collection. Then, through careful analysis, determine whether the information obtained corroborate one another. If so, this provides a great deal more validity and reliability for the data collected and should help ensure the accuracy of the Job Task Analysis results. Once you have defined each of the individual tasks required of any given job or position, critical decisions can be made internally about how to go about filling the position. Unfortunately, many organizations today still do not complete a formal Job Task Analysis, but simply take old job descriptions and modify them prior to advertising or posting a position based off of intuition and tradition. The obvious problem with this is that many times these job descriptions are based upon what the job has become due to internal and external influences, office politics, unrealistic expectations, or even perceptions, and not necessarily what the job or position duties and responsibilities really consist of in today's fast paced and ever-changing world. In fact, many job descriptions are wrought with legally challengeable and indefensible requirements and expectations and are lacking the specific identification of the real competencies required for success in a specific position. I would like to finish this discussion by proposing that it isn't always what skill set you possess or the attributes of your resume that make you successful; it is your willingness to use those skills, knowledge, and abilities that really counts towards one's success, hence the criticality of hiring the right people for the right job!

With this same thought in mind, the hiring of the right people is one of the most interesting and challenging tasks involved in the HR process today. Recruiting and selecting the right personnel for your team is critically important to the successful start of the entire HR process. One of the very first decisions to be made regarding recruiting the right talent is to determine if the position in question requires an entry level applicant, someone with an advanced skill set, or possibly even hiring someone from the outside using lateral entry. Many times, this is a philosophical issue to be addressed by top management, due to the positive and negative repercussions that may arise by "going outside" the current organizational structure to find someone for the position in question. With changing attitudes toward our careers today, many Americans view their jobs differently, and with this have come a wide variety of new attitudes on staffing positions and the work/life balance as a whole. There are ideas as simple as job-sharing, using retirees as consultants, hiring part-time employees, using more contractors, using volunteers, and even developing lists of reservists such as the military does, thus enabling you to better tap the varying skill sets and diversity of the available employee workforce for your business. Regardless of how you decide to fill a position, there are specific skill sets and personality traits that should be considered as you commence with identifying both philosophically and tangibly what types of individuals can best fulfill the needs of the organization.

A few examples of the various skill sets and personality traits to consider:

- Technical skill set
- Personality traits
- Character traits
- Personal demographics, such as race, ethnicity, culture, traditions & customs, gender, geographical traits, etc.
- Experience level
- Languages spoken
- Advanced education and training levels
- Reputation and credibility in the field
- Ability to connect, develop alliances, network with others, and form partnerships.
- Past performance levels and performance appraisal results

Regardless of whomever you decide to bring into the organization, there are a wide variety of very important steps to effectively and successfully recruiting, assimilating, growing, and retaining the right individual as part of the organization. So many times, in the past, and even today, organizations of every type fail to find the right employees and team members who possess the various skills, knowledge, abilities, and standards of performance the organization expects, thus again, reinforcing the criticality of effective human resources and talent management practices today!

SECTION 4

Plan Implementation through Strategic Management

CHAPTER 9

MANAGE PROCESSES EFFECTIVELY, INCLUDING THE CHANGE MANAGEMENT PROCESS!

Plan thoroughly and prepare for the effective execution of the plan, and remember to successfully manage the change required by the organization.

Like the Pareto 80/20 Principle, developing the strategic plan comprises only 20% of your time in the entire strategic planning and management process. The real herculean effort in all of this is managing the implementation of the plan, which accounts for the other 80% of time and effort. Strategic management, or "managing the process" of the plan's implementation, obviously requires a great many proven and time-tested principles and practices. These practices can be found in the sciences of organizational behavior and development, operations management, organizational management, and even industrial psychology, just to name a few. We will discuss them at length in the following two chapters. For example, both organizational management and systems theory use a great many principles, processes, and tools to ensure that everything gets done correctly, in the right order, to the right standard and in a timely fashion.

Applying these principles during operations in the field requires specific methods and tools such as:

- Work Breakdown Structures
- Decision Analysis methods such as Decision Trees and Critical Path Analyses
- Tables of Organizations with well delineated Chains of Command and Spans of Controls
- Well defined and realistic budget processes, such as Zero-based Budgeting
- Performance assessment measures such as the effective use of annual performance appraisals
- Pay for performance structures, matrix and tables

All of the above-mentioned tools are designed to help ensure the effective administration, operation, and support of the organization and its many processes as it works towards accomplishing the goals and objectives agreed upon and accepted in the strategic plan. Of course, as the organization accomplishes its identified mission, there are by-products which naturally occur, such as inter-office alliances, office politics, productivity, conflict, and of course change.

Change is a naturally occurring by-product of any organization that is moving forward towards the accomplishment of its mission and vision. The key to effective change is to ensure that it is proactive and planned for change, which has been forecasted or anticipated and is actually helping to move the organization forward. Unplanned for, and unpredicted change is many times considered negative in nature and can actually be a barrier, or at least a distraction to the organization accomplishing its "Big 5 measures of success" discussed earlier. Merle Switzer, a nationally recognized change management expert states there are 5 major steps to building a "Commitment for Change."

The 5 steps are as follows:

Step 1) Identify whose commitment is needed.

Step 2) Determine the level of commitment needed.

Step 3) Estimate the critical mass needed.

Step 4) Get the commitment of the critical mass.

Step 5) Status check to monitor the real level of commitment.

Dr. Switzer states that building commitment takes creative, well accepted and understandable change, time, and lastly energy from those who will both drive the change and those who will have to accept the change. He also states that a little effort up front certainly leverages the odds in favor of lessening the resistance from those affected by the change. Another expert in the field of change is of course Dr. John Kotter, who in his 2002 book, *The Heart of Change*, espouses to there being a total of eight steps to ensuring that meaningful and long-lasting change takes effect. Dr. Kotter states that the following steps should be taken for successful large-scale change to be successful.

Dr. Kotter's 8 steps are as follows:

Step 1 – Increase urgency.

Step 2 – Build the guiding team.

Step 3 – Get the vision right.

Step 4 – Communicate for buy-in.

Step 5 – Empower action.

Step 6 – Create short-term wins.

Step 7 – Don't let up.

Step 8 – Make the change stick.

Dr. Kotter concludes that not only are these steps critical to the institutionalization of change, but that we should always remember there are many times overlap between these stages, and that due to the complexity of the world we work in today, that each step is not necessarily always required for success, based upon the type of situation faced. Again, we learn that with change, just as with all processes in a complicated world, requires a great deal of flexibility! We should conclude with the fact that unplanned negative change can place large amounts of anxiety and stress on both the members of the organization and also on the processes and systems found within the organization. Either of which will undoubtedly have a negative impact on the organization's effectiveness and success. It would behoove all of us as we move our organization's forward to embrace change as needed particularly in this ever-changing world we work and live in, but at the same time try to minimize the frustration that can accompany unwanted or unplanned for change!

CHAPTER 10

USE YOUR ORGANZIATIONAL MANAGEMNT TOOLS EFFECTIVELY AND ALWAYS CONTINUE TO LIMIT RISK TO THE ORGANIZATION!

Utilize proven Organizational Management principles and standardized business practices to maximize efficiency and effectiveness throughout your team and the organization.

To some people today, the many, seemingly mundane tasks associated with the management of an organization, may not appear to be flashy or even a major priority. That may be because many of the typical standardized business practices and management functions do not necessarily possess the glamor or allure that television and other social media outlets have presented them as possibly being. However, as anyone who has ever held a management or leadership position realizes these various functions are absolutely critical to the efficient operation and administration of any organization, regardless of its structure, type or mission.

Possessing a vision for the organization, setting the direction, and motivating others to perform to their fullest can indeed sound like a daunting task. Even something as simple as scheduling activities and events requires planning and the ability to forecast and predict the order in which functions must be accomplished. The proper scheduling of various activities is indeed important because many tasks must be accomplished in a very specific order if they are to be helpful in accomplishing the organization's mission. If the sequencing of activities is completed incorrectly, a wide variety of negative effects and byproducts can occur. Managing the process of these various activities is critical to being a successful manager and leader. A perfect example of this can be found in General, and later President, Dwight D. Eisenhower. At the beginning of World War II, he was living a fairly typical life as a mid-level military officer in the Unites States Army, without much hope for advancement and with no real purpose to his career. In fact, at one point during the 1930s he actually discussed with his wife resigning his commission from the Army and going back to farming in Pennsylvania. Thankfully for both the Unites States and our Allies in Europe, he decided not to. Eisenhower's ability to relate to others, form trusting and long-lasting relationships as a member of a team, and bring about consensus in various groups, coupled with his skill at many of the management practices discussed throughout this text, helped him experience a meteoric rise through the ranks of the U.S. Army, and ultimately become the Supreme Allied Commander of the Allied forces fighting in Europe during World War II. All of this came from a man who had very limited experience in actual combat, or leading troops into battle of any sort, but had experience in many of the behind-the-scenes tasks associated with being a great organizer and manager. It is indeed obvious, that the execution of every task contained within the strategic plan requires sound Organizational Management practices be utilized if success is to ever be realized.

Some of the more prevalent and widely accepted Organizational Management practices in use today are presented below.

Planning	Organizing	Directing	Controlling
Coordinating	Sequencing	Scheduling	Staffing
Delegating	Budgeting	Communicating	Assigning
Disciplining	Training	Assessing	Hiring

The many functions, processes, and tasks that must be completed on a daily basis in order to effectively implement the strategic plan for the organization, requires the identification of a leader who will be responsible for ensuring that each specific task gets both accomplished and in the right order. This delegation of tasks, however, must happen at two levels within the organization: the various tasks themselves must be completed by some member of the employee workforce, while simultaneously being directed, supervised, and inspected by a member of management. As you may now assume, we will be discussing both task execution and accountability in this chapter and how absolutely important the proper delineation of tasks is, if anything is to ever be accomplished in an exemplary fashion. This requires a system's approach to operating a high performing organization. The effective coordination required of the administrative, operational, and support functions within the organization requires a well-orchestrated and comprehensive description of the responsibility and accountability required for the successful accomplishment of each task identified within the strategic plan. The accomplishment of every daily, operational, administrative, and support task required of the strategic plan's implementation must meet the dual criteria of being both efficient and effective. Otherwise, organizational success will most assuredly be compromised. You may recognize some of the following items as being similar to the standards required of a performance objective, as we defined their identifying characteristics earlier in the strategic planning process chapter. For performance objectives to be successful they must be SMART: Specific, Measurable, Attainable, Realistic, and Timely. When we implement the organization's strategic plan on a daily basis, we are executing each of these organizational objectives at very specific locations, standards and levels within the organization. The tasks associated with each of the already identified and agreed upon organizational objectives, must now be successfully completed by an individual employee or team and supervised by a member of the organization's supervisory management cadre, to ensure standards of productivity, service, quality, cutting waste, running lean, and risk management standards are being adhered to. The execution of each major task grouping should be spelled out in detail during each employee's annual written performance appraisal and then supervised by a member of the organization's supervisory management team, once daily, tactical plans are decided upon and rolled out.

A further explanation of each point of a SMART objective can be found below:

- **Specific** – in detail to ensure the employee knows what standard they must meet.
- **Measurable** – "what gets measured gets done" and employees must know to what degree or priority does this task fall amongst all of the rest of the tasks within their span of control or area of responsibility.
- **Attainable** – Does the employee have the skills, knowledge and ability to complete the identified tasks to the "work performance standard" provided?
- **Realistic** – Has the organization provided the employee with the necessary resources required to effectively and efficiently meet the work performance standards of this specific task

including time, funding, technology, assistance, processes, supervision required.

- **Timely** – Is this specific task being completed in the proper sequence and within the required time limits for it to be considered successfully executed? Timing can be and many times is everything when trying to complete a complicated task within the designated work design structure.

As we can see, the accomplishment of specific tasks by specific team members within the organization requires that these performance objectives meet the same SMART requirements that the organization's objectives do, as identified in the strategic plan.

Having said that, they must also adhere to the following "Big 5" measures of performance, and organizational success:

Production standards – the number of tasks required to maintain or meet the organization's identified work performance standards for production levels.

Service to Customers, Clients, and Colleagues – the level of service to any stakeholder, including processing data, providing correct and factual information, answering questions, and solving problems in a timely and courteous manner commensurate with the work performance standards of the organization.

Quality Control and Assurance - is an obvious requirement of the execution of any tasks within an organization. Increased levels of productivity and/or responsiveness as a delegator of various stakeholders' requests will be in vain if the level of quality suffers. The cost of poor-quality control can be insurmountable for an organization, due to the ripple effect it can quickly have!

Poor-quality control can result in any one of the following negative byproducts:

- Criminal prosecution or civil litigation
- Required recalls
- Major workflow and process adjustments
- Increasing employee frustration levels coupled with declines in performance.
- Contract violations resulting in penalties and fewer renewals.
- Loss of reputation for the organization, resulting in both fewer first-time sales and returning sales.
- Decreased ability to recruit and meet future workforce requirements.
- Inability to retain current work force.

Cutting Waste and Running Lean – many organizations today, particularly non-profits and government entities, must cut waste wherever and whenever possible. Every event, effort, or activity must be accompanied by a comprehensive cost-benefit analysis. Running lean and using one's resources wisely is also part of this effort, to cut waste by ensuring you utilize every resource effectively. This is a perfect example as to why many organizations in the public sector utilize Zero-based Budgeting, or at least some form of a modified Zero-based Budget, where each expenditure must be justified as to how it helps the organization fulfill its identified mission.

Risk Mitigation and Management – As can be seen by the schematic on page 64, risk management is a critical process today and involves all of the 5 P's. The development of appropriate policies, procedures, processes, practices, and progress tracking methods will help ensure your organization and all of its team members follow the rules. Risk management is not always about the possibility of being held statutorily or civilly liable for some type of ethical or legal transgression. In today's world we must all view risk management in a larger perspective. Risk management today involves identifying anything that inhibits or endangers the organization from being able to fulfill its mission and vision. We are all risk managers, and we must all identify anything that stands in the way of our organization's success.

Some examples of risks that cause concern about an organization's internal efficiency and effectiveness are as follows:

- Failure to delegate
- Incomplete information or lack of intelligence
- Ineffective communication
- Inadequate funding
- Poor talent management
- Inoperable information technology
- Indecision or procrastination
- Poor conflict management
- Lack of diversity at multiple levels
- Continual crisis management
- Mission Creep and too many priorities
- Duplication of effort or redundancy
- Inept leadership

Obviously, the list goes on and on, but I believe anyone can see that the number of internal risks to the organization's success is both long and significant and must be taken seriously. The costs of poor-quality control are critical to an organization's success or failure. As we conclude the importance of initially identifying and maintaining accountability within the organization, never underestimate the last two pieces to organizational responsibility, which is to cut waste and continue increasing efficiency through managing risk whenever and wherever possible. We live in a world where competition for resources and the desire to increase or grow the bottom line through containing and controlling costs is the "call of the day." Being held accountable for implementing the cost-controlling methods already in use by the organization and identifying new methods of cutting costs and saving money are critical. With this in mind, you will find the risk management model which will assist you as you attempt to identify and effectively address various risks in your organization.

The Warren – **5 Ps of Risk Management Model**

Identify past, current or future problems, issues and concerns –

Develop POLICY to outline and guide behavior to address the above -

Develop PROCEDURES to effectively implement the policy -

Design PROCESSES to implement the procedures -

PRACTICE the policy, procedures and processes outlined above -

Assess PROGRESS regularly -

Lastly, all of the major tenets and principles on accountability already presented in this chapter are additional methods for identifying risk to the organization. They serve as a reminder of just how important every single person is to preventing risk, mitigating the negative impacts those risks bring to the organization, and maintaining sustainability in a very competitive world. These principles simply reaffirm the need for every member of an organization, from entry level employee to top leadership, to understand that risk management is everyone's responsibility. If risks are not identified and addressed early on, they may very well become a crisis in the future. Whether the risk is internal or external, the cost can be catastrophic to both individual team members and the organization.

Remember, "What gets measured gets done." Without explicit and well-delineated responsibility for each and every task included in the strategic plan, one cannot expect there to be effective accountability. Consequently, limited accountability may of course equate to poor performance and an inability to successfully accomplish the "Big 5" measures of organizational success presented above. Even a lack of urgency on the part of individual employees, or systemic barriers to organizational success such as embedded time and energy wasters, can facilitate the beginning of the end for those organizations that are already weakened or complacent due to the presence of various, unaddressed risks or uncontrolled variables!

CHAPTER 11

BUILD EFFECTIVE SYSTEMS AND PROCESSES THAT WORK!!

Design and utilize accepted Operations Management, and Systems Theory principles and concepts to help ensure success.

One of the most critical concepts for leaders and personnel to understand today is why integrating Operations Management processes and practices into a cohesive system or systems within the organization is so important to organizational success. But before we discuss the criticality of how we must engage in the effective use of many of the most basic Operations Management principles in order to succeed as an organization, we must first settle on a working definition of Operations Management. There are many formal definitions of Operations Management dating back to the Hawthorne Studies and Frederick Taylor, who is considered by many to be the father of scientific management. However, what today's organizations require is a more flexible definition of Operations Management.

Operational Management entails designing, developing, aligning, and resourcing the functions and entities of the organization in order to successfully implement its strategic plan and ultimately accomplish its mission. Therefore, it is imperative that leadership at every level of the organization design and utilize the most effective policies, processes, procedures, practices and methods to assist every member of the organization in executing the tasks required of them. From completing job task analyses, to determining what types of skillsets and personality types are required for a specific job or position, to writing policies that provide guidance to supervisors and employees as they execute their various duties, the principles of Operations Management are utilized continuously. Designing an organization, managing that organization, continuously and consistently setting direction, providing guidance, removing obstacles, allowing for individual growth, encouraging creativity and innovation, and rewarding performance, are just a few examples of the management principles and practices considered part of effective Operations Management.

Bringing it all together by initiating the use of sound Operations Management and integrated systems theory and principles, to support administrative, operational, and support services of all types is a must for high performance today. These are not single, stand-alone functions, processes, or procedures, but rather part of the many larger organizational systems required for success. Together they constitute a series of very complicated and complex functions, processes, and procedures designed in such a fashion as to maximize the efficiency and synergy of the resources available to the organization. Operations Management also focuses on the interrelatedness and cross-functionality of individuals, teams, business units, and other organization-wide entities. In fact, later in this chapter, the concept of Integrated Strategic Management Systems and their importance to organizational high performance and success will be discussed in detail. Organizations must be designed, organized, and operated to tactically execute each of the tasks identified in the strategic plan. This concept can best be described in the adage "think strategically" and "act tactically", if we ever hope to limit the frustration that can many times accompany working with various complicated processes and systems!

The best analogy I can provide for the criticality of systems to organizational success, is to consider a single singer or a single musician; by themselves they are indeed talented and provide their audience with delightful and entertaining music, but even with that, compare them to a composer who has put to paper the music for an entire orchestra, coordinating a wide variety of musical instruments in time with each other. Then add in the conductor, other performers, and perhaps actors and back-stage workers. Everyone has a well-defined job in order for the composer's music to be brought to life with as much depth of feeling and impact as possible. By now this description of the operations of an orchestra should be reminding you of an organization's strategic plan. It must be designed and developed strategically, yet implemented daily by each team member, if the organization's mission is to be realized. One key point here is the critical nature of great leadership to effective Operations Management. If top leadership does not drive the development of the strategic plan, then there will be no standardized sheet of music from which to play. Also, if leadership fails to seek both input and feedback in the strategic plan development process, it will certainly lack "buy-in," with many team members possibly becoming uncommitted or unwilling to work as directed. It should be quite obvious, that from the CEO, CFO, and COO, down to the most entry-level employee or temporary contractor, everyone must know their duties and responsibilities and be held accountable for the implementation of their part of the organization's strategic plan, otherwise, the entire effort will ultimately fail.

The need for systems: Trying to align and harness the many entities, functions, and processes utilized by the organization is indeed critical for organizational success. Every effort must be made to increase productivity, service levels, quality control and assurance, cutting waste and running lean, and even mitigating risks, if the organization ever hopes to attain its potential level of performance. A systems approach is mandatory for any organization attempting to become great. The typical organization possesses so many physical entities, functions, processes, policies, procedures, resources, and talent, etc., that it is sometimes hard to fathom trying to succeed without utilizing various comprehensive systems today. All organizations, as they grow in size and complexity, certainly require more well-developed and mature processes and systems.

The largest and most complicated variable in any organization is the human component and the various personality traits and skillsets that accompany each individual team member. Trying to convince every employee to work in a unified manner towards an agreed upon vision for the betterment of the organization most certainly requires a systems approach. Well-developed systems help ensure that proper resources are in place and that the right personnel are in their most effective position within the organization. The synergy that teamwork produces by using a systems approach within the organization cannot be accurately measured or fully appreciated. Therefore, there must be a pragmatic approach utilized in the designing, developing and implementation of the many working systems required of success.

Because of the tremendous need for a systems approach to organizational performance and success, the author in 2011 developed the concept of the Integrated Strategic Management System (ISMS). It was first unveiled in Police Chief Magazine in March of 2012 in an article entitled, "Is Your Organization an Integrated Strategic Management System?" Since then, the author has espoused that there are more organizations out there today than ever before, which continue to fail to work as well-designed and high performing systems. Some organizations are designed so poorly that they have morphed or evolved into entities where internal competition is fostered and a complete lack of cooperation exists. That organizations today with this type of toxic leadership, which allow negative organizational cultures to develop and exist is alarming. In response, we as leaders must understand the true value of working within a systems approach. The call of the day must be: "When we win, I win, and when I win, we all win." This is in fact what teamwork, synergy and organizational success is all about!

Determining whether or not your organization works as an Integrated Strategic Management System, or ISMS, is the first step in making the decision to complete an organizational analysis. Such an analysis determines if you already work as a system, and if not, where you need to start making changes to ensure you do. The ISMS takes the current organizational analysis and design process well beyond what almost every other similar analysis engages in today. As Jim Collins expressed in his 2001 book "Good to Great," concentrating simply on the organizational structure and the more obvious functions of the organization is not enough to identify the changes needed to drive an organization towards excellence. Many proactive organizations that already engage in a formalized annual strategic planning process also engage in an annual organizational analysis as part of their strategic planning effort, hence why many at least engage in some type of SWOT analysis and Gap analysis as part of their annual planning process. However, a truly comprehensive study of the organization – required as one of the first steps in designing an ISMS – should concentrate its analyses on all administrative, operational, and support services areas, including the various business practices, production, and service-oriented functions of the organization. For example, internal competition, inefficiency, redundancy of effort, and conflict can quickly boil over into heightened competition between operational field units, which can result in a variety of very negative tangible issues for the organization such as: poor individual and team performance, increased wastes, misdirected efforts, overlooked priorities, and increased risk and liability.

Organizations must complete a comprehensive organizational analysis to determine exactly who, what, where, when, why, how, and to what degree these dysfunctional relationships and processes exist. They must then set in motion a plan to redesign the entire organization into a well-defined, highly performing integrated system or ISMS. Integrating and utilizing the best practices of both the private and public sectors, culminating in a well-designed system, coupled with great leadership and a well-defined and agreed-upon vision and strategic plan, can result in an organization experiencing tremendous growth in each of the "Big 5" measures of success. This philosophical change should result in the organization learning to concentrate on the more important, impact focused outcomes of the organization, and not on the more obvious and less effective outputs currently tracked and measured by so many organizations today. Identifying, designing, and developing a completely new approach — or at the very least a redesigned, more holistic, systemic approach to the organization's administrative functions and operations—should result in a convergence of the synergy required for your organization to remain viable, sustainable, and appropriately positioned for success well into the 21st century.

The goal of OM and systems theory is to maximize the 3 Positive Cs of cooperation, communication, and collaboration, rather than internal competition, conflict and chaos. The most critical risk to any organization is not from competitors on the outside, but rather from "not getting the most out of your employee workforce and fellow team members" on the inside. Many of the above-mentioned frustrations and stressors are generated not by the organization's mission itself, but by the lack of appropriate policy, procedures, processes, practices, poor or inept leadership, dysfunctional relationships amongst employees and supervisors and other organizational stakeholders straying from the mission, and of course but not lastly poorly functioning systems. For instance, leadership and talent management are many times relational in nature and based in great part on the many attributes and idiosyncrasies of the people who make these processes move and "go". The cooperation, collaboration, and communication you would automatically think exists in all organizations is many times lacking today. In fact, in some organizations, competition and conflict seem to be the call of day; I don't mean external competition by one's most obvious competitors, but as stated above, unhealthy internal competition that acts as a major distraction within the organization. Dr. Michael Hammer in his book *The Agenda*, explains that "being easy to do business with" is critical to organizational success today. One might conclude that he is discussing the need for being more customer-focused or customer-centric, but if we look one step further, we begin to understand that he actually means all members of an organization must be willing and capable of working together internally for the betterment of the team and the organization as a whole.

There is only one way to ensure that an organization will experience the success that the strategic plan intended and that is through the use of Integrated Strategic Management Systems. I learned early on as a leader in various organizations and also as a college professor, just how limited many people's knowledge is regarding the critical nature of systems to their organization's success. What I found was that a great many students had studied the required courses from the specific business or leadership development course curriculums they had chosen to pursue, but when they were asked to provide a more comprehensive analysis of how an organization actually worked, they could not figure out how all of the pieces fit together or interacted effectively. If instructors do not take the time or make the effort to provide these young, inexperienced students with a comprehensive picture of how to achieve the long-term strategic goals and objectives of their organization, they will be unable to link together what they have learned in each of the many different business disciplines and courses they have studied. The Warren Integrated Strategic Management System, (ISMS) provides students with both a schematic and detailed description of how each of the functions of the typical organization must work together if success is to be realized. After a great deal of research and several renditions, the current concept of the ISMS has been met with tremendous success. Several articles and numerous presentations have since been made on the criticality of systems and the effective management of processes and the critical role they both play in realizing organizational success today.

Below are the critical components and steps to the current comprehensive ISMS model:

Step 1 – Develop the strategic plan.

Step 2 – Identify and develop each of the policies, procedures, processes, practices and progress measures required for strategic plan implementation.

Step 3 – Resource the plan, including funding, equipment, supplies, raw materials, technology requirements etc.

Step 4 – Recruit, onboard and train the necessary human resources and talent required for plan implementation.

Step 5 – Identify and develop all of the outside contacts required for success. from developing partnerships, marketing plans, political contacts to other potential stakeholders.

Step 6 – Implement the plan and execute the identified strategies and tasks required for successful accomplishment of the organization's mission.

Step 7 – Continually access progress and make adjustments when necessary.

Step 8 – Communicate your progress and success to all organizational stakeholders.

Many organizations still operate with a more traditional, fragmented approach, full of divergence and independence in thought and action, between various administrative, operational, and support functions. Organizational entities working independently of each other detract from an organization's attempt to identify and communicate a "shared vision" for the organization. Many executives today are realizing the value that reinventing, or at least reorganizing, their various entities can have on overall effectiveness—from very specific changes such as the New Jersey State Police intelligence-led policing initiative, post-9/11; to November 2011, when the Houston, Texas, Police Department received its ISO 9000:2008 certification for process improvement and quality assurance. One of the largest single examples of an intentional, well-designed, and fully implemented organizational transformation with an ISMS as its mainstay, was the U.S. Coast Guard, under the direction of former Commandant Admiral Thad Allen. Under Admiral Allen's leadership, the Coast Guard was tasked with redesigning its entire organizational structure, operational processes, and business model for increased efficiency and interoperability. The idea of joining the best of both the private and public sector's business practices—coupled with strong, proven, operational methodologies—is not a new concept; however, it certainly deserves revisiting from a completely new perspective: that of transforming an organization into a comprehensive and fully operational ISMS, as shown above.

Every member or employee in the organization's workforce, from entry-level to chief executive, should consider regularly studying the organization for areas where functions or processes can be streamlined, redesigned, or transformed into something better. From identifying external risks, to internally engaging in more fortuitous human resources management practices, to reallocating overtime funds for greater impact, areas where risks or inefficiency exist should be quickly identified and addressed.

Once the chief executive and their leadership team has committed to this new philosophy of advanced Operations Management, the challenge becomes assembling the appropriate team that can study, design, plan, and facilitate the implementation of the ISMS within the organization. This will, in turn, help in developing a new, high-performing organization that is capable of operating as a fully functioning, integrated system. The internal team designated for this task should have expertise in both Operations and Organizational Management, and also understand the criticality of these areas to the organization's overall success.

Some of these critical areas are listed below:

- Strategic planning and the strategic management process.
- Operations Management processes.
- Leadership philosophy styles and supervisory management practices.
- Evidence-based decision making, utilizing the latest available business intelligence, driven by current and accurate data, information and intelligence.
- Effective human resources and talent management functions.
- Funding and budget processes.
- IT and MIS integration and interoperability.

An effective Integrated Strategic Management System (ISMS) is predicated on blending these concepts into a well-designed and well-orchestrated strategic plan. As the team conducts this in-depth organizational analysis, with commensurate recommendations for the redesign of the organization's various functions, they should concentrate their initial efforts on identifying the typical symptoms associated with most organizational problems.

Some possible areas to concentrate their analysis efforts on include:

- Poor business practices.
- Lack of written policies or conflicting policies and standard operating procedures.

- Lack of required skill sets by employee workforce.
- Redundancy of effort.
- Areas of undue risks experienced.
- Ethical transgressions and violations of the rules and regulations.
- Poor morale
- Mission creep
- Inefficiencies in effort
- Conflicting priorities
- Major personality conflicts
- Areas of disruptive or aggressive internal competition.
- Poor individual or team performance levels.
- Areas of increased costs and waste.

To no surprise, research reveals that many organizations are not designed for working well as interdependent systems. Many organizations have individuals or entities competing against each other and sometimes even engaging in outright conflict, either administratively or operationally. Administrative functions and processes, along with the many operational and support services of the organization, should work in unison toward the accomplishment of the organization's overall mission. These processes designed, implemented, and led in a strong, forward-leaning, forward-thinking, high-performance organization can achieve extraordinary levels of performance and success. If agencies and organizations operate with a systems approach, they can find great utility and functionality, even in instances where an organization wants to change its entire operational philosophy. For example, when the chief of the Jackson Police Department in Michigan decided to transform the organization's traditional policing philosophy to one of community policing, the organization quickly realized that a major change in methodologies and philosophy would require the transformation of the entire organization, not just the addition of a unit or assigning of extra responsibilities to specific individuals or entities. This desire to change the focus and priorities of the Jackson Police Department offered the Chief the perfect opportunity to transform the entire organization into a fully operational Integrated Strategic Management System.

The study, design, and use of organizations as Integrated Strategic Management Systems, or (ISMS), brings together the best leadership, systems theory, and Operations Management practices available in the United States today. Ensuring that organizations work as well-designed systems has been proven to be a more productive and effective way to accomplish both an organization's mission and vision. Proven processes and methods of effective and successful Operations Management are within every forward-thinking organization's reach. The most important challenge to overcome before this type of efficiency and effectiveness can be realized in mass, is that every level of leadership and every member of the employee workforce must both understand and believe in the incredible potential this type of applied strategic management can not only have on the organization in the short term, but also be willing to use these same principles to help move the organization forward successfully into the 21st century!

SECTION 5

Leadership, High Performance and Following the Plan!

CHAPTER 12

LEADERS IGNITE ENTHUSIASM AND MOTIVATE OTHERS!

Understand the true value of motivated employees, ensuring a high quality of work life and work life balance, and recognizing the "true costs of low morale".

E veryone talks about high performing teams and how important teamwork is to accomplishing specific projects and the organization's overall goals. No one will argue with the previous statement; however, we might first want to understand the criticality of individual high performance to obtaining and maintaining both high team and organizational performance levels. Superior performers, and not just the "average joes," are what all organizations strive to fill their ranks with, because one high performer may be as valuable as many regular employees in certain situations. Leadership is all about identifying each individual team member's specific personality traits, character traits, skills, knowledge base, abilities, and professional goals, in an effort to help that employee perform to their absolute best. Do that, and they will continue to excel, not just when you are around, but also when you are not. This is the key tenet to voluntary followership and high performance, however it still begs the question of how do I as a leader, convince people to follow me, not because they have to, but because they realize that it is good for all parties involved, including both them and the organization as a whole? This is a good time to remind all of us that accomplishing the goals and objectives of the organization through the identified and agreed upon strategies stated in the strategic plan, is "what it is all about," this elusive "thing" called performance! So, putting all theory, concepts, principles, and models aside, what it all boils down to is effective leadership influencing other individuals and team members in a positive fashion, in an effort to get the very best performance possible from everyone!

Most experts agree that increasing an employee's job satisfaction, fulfillment and opportunities for growth normally equates to higher morale, but it is dangerous to always assume this. See, this simple and widely agreed upon tenet assumes that every employee is intrinsically motivated to perform higher. I think this idea has become very popular in recent years, because it has become taboo to insinuate or even agree with the idea that some people are motivated extrinsically more than intrinsically. Let's face it; some people are in it for the money, or a wide variety of other very tangible motivators. For example, a simple challenging economy, such as we have had in recent years in the United States, can cause tangible motivators to become more enticing. By reviewing Maslow's Hierarchy of Needs, we could argue all day about how to accurately define what motivates an individual to perform a certain task, to a certain level, in a certain situation.

One widely accepted motivational theory today is Vroom's Expectancy Theory. Vroom postulates that every employee has specific expectations of the organization and its leadership when they join it, and that as long as those expectations continue to be met, then the employee's motivation to perform will remain high. This is not always the case though, because as we all know, there are many examples of where the employee fails to meet the organization's expectations for performance and thus the symbiotic relationship between the two begins to deteriorate. This type of situation can occur in any organization due to a wide variety of hard to control, independent variables. It can also most assuredly be expedited, when an employee's values do not align well with those of the organization or its leadership. This lack of "career congruency" can cause the positive relationship that once existed to dissipate quickly, or even disintegrate all together.

Motivation really boils down to identifying what it is that motivates a person to perform highly, regardless of their age, socioeconomic status, position in the company, educational level, race, etc. and then focusing on those individual values and needs. There are so many genetic-based personality traits, experienced-based norms, societal and cultural values, and even environmental factors impacting this equation that no one could ever possibly identify all of the independent variables influencing each and every one of us, and what makes us "who we are." Many employees today are asking themselves the following questions: Who am I? Why am I here? and Do I make a difference? I think we all know by now, or at least you do if you have been in the job of leading others for any length of time, that every single person who works for you, requires a very specific and detailed career development plan to assist them in achieving their personal and professional goals in life and at work. Similar to an IEP or Individualized Educational Program, an individual's career development plan should be very specific and tailored to the needs of that particular employee.

All other factors aside, a major variable on how employees feel about work comes from their interactions with and perceptions of their direct supervisors and managers, including the commensurate leadership styles those individuals utilize. One's leadership style is incredibly important to everyone's performance and the organization's overall success. The power of emotion in the workplace is an incredible influencer on people and hence the reason for what the author terms "the myth of rational leadership." If leadership was rational, then we would be able to identify a possible formula for effectively leading others in various situations and under varying circumstances. This is why the leadership formula discussed in subsequent chapters is so appropriate in developing followership in others. You have to get to know what makes others "tick," and that cannot be done without communicating with them on a regular basis and in a positive manner. In fact, negative communications and interactions could possibly cause your ability to identify what is really important, or motivating to the individual employee, to become even more arduous. If we communicate well with our fellow team members, we will "get to know them" and when we get to know them, we will begin to identify what is really important to them personally and professionally. Once this has been accomplished, we can work towards providing our team members with what it is that brings out and accentuates their very best performance in the workplace.

By now you should be saying, "well this whole discussion is nothing but common sense", and anyone could do this if they wanted to. If that was the case, why then are we spending billions of dollars every year in the United States to provide leadership training and education in a variety of different venues and modalities for both current and future members of the employee workforce? Some leaders want to lead, but can't get it together, while others can lead, but don't want to, or refuse to. Still others continue to believe in and lead in very archaic styles, such as motivating employees by force, coercion, or threat. We all know what this traditional "autocratic" leadership style produces – short-term results with absolutely no allegiance to either you, the team, or the agreed upon vision of the organization and the strategic plan. This leads to a lack of long-term motivation to perform, particularly when you or the acting supervisor are not present. How much productivity, quality control, and service do we in American industry and government lose due to our archaic methods of leading others and conducting business as usual? Leadership is relational and because of this, building positive relationships is our only hope of guaranteeing long-term high performance in our organizations today!

Leadership is all about providing or engaging in effective talent management and getting others to want to voluntarily work hard towards the organization's goals, objectives, and mission. All administrative, operational, and support functions throughout the organization, should understand the importance of Performance-Based Results (PBR) management and how important "managing the process" is for the successful implementation of the strategic plan. The results of a recent survey of business executives from throughout the country revealed that their employees' failure to execute tasks is one of the most critical issues faced by them as executives today. The best plans, whether tactical or strategic in nature, are of little use if your personnel fail to execute those plans when required.

Two critical questions I ask when studying specific human performance issues are, which of the two following statements, if either, are present, and if so, how prevalent or to what degree?

They **Can** Perform well – But **Won't** = **Discipline** Issue

They **Want** to Perform well – But **Can't** = **Training** Issue

When there is a lack of performance, ask the following questions:

- Do we know who?
- Do we know what?
- Do we know how much?

- Do we know when?
- Do we know where?

and most importantly,

- Do we know why?

What we seek to know is why employees who have successfully performed certain tasks in the past now refuse to perform the task correctly or to the expected work performance standard. Many times, this equates to a lack of motivation on the part of the employee to perform the identified task. As a supervisor, you must investigate and identify the reasoning behind the employee's failure to perform. Is there a lack of urgency? Poor time management? Passive resistance? Or even sabotage? In today's world, it could also be poor engagement, lack of concentration, failure to focus, or refusal to put forth the emotional labor required of the task or position. The leadership response to this issue could take the form of progressive discipline, and, if it continues or prolongs itself, could ultimately result in termination. The second situation that could cause a lack of performance on the part of your personnel could be a lack of skill or ability due to poor education or training. This situation, if diagnosed as the problem, can many times be adequately addressed or corrected. At this point the decision should be made as to whether the proper training or retraining is cost effective and worth attempting, based upon how serious the perceived deficiency actually is. Most supervisors, when interviewed about poor performance on the part of their employees, almost always agree they would rather have someone who wants to do something but can't, than someone who can, but refuses to! This is primarily because the headaches of dealing with a discipline issue are much more pronounced than simply providing an opportunity for training. One must always remember that the number one responsibility of supervision is to initiate and/or change behavior. Changing a member of your employee workforce's behavior due to a training deficiency is certainly going to be less painful than initiating discipline in an attempt to change behavior.

Finally, one of the last items that needs to be addressed as we discuss the lack of execution on the part of so many employees today, is the question of what role time management plays in these types of situations. I believe, after years of working with employee's time management issues, that we overgeneralize the problem. It isn't really a time management issue so much as the lack of a sense of urgency on the part of the employee. There are many people today who lack the self-discipline to generate an original sense of urgency; therefore, they do not recognize the need to self-initiate action on certain tasks in a timely manner, and many times require some type of outside influence to force them to move on the activities in question. I believe the procrastination being displayed by some employees today in various businesses and organizations is in fact approaching epidemic levels. What is even more critical to the overall performance equation, and the negative impact this mentality and or personality trait has on performance, is the negative domino effect it has on others in the system, and even the organization as a whole. When someone procrastinates and waits until the last minute to engage in an activity or is running late in the execution of their assigned tasks, there is a negative ripple effect on others who are now rushed, due to the time constraints placed upon them by the procrastinator. Unfortunately, the negative impact on others due to this lack of urgency and failure to perform is sometimes irreversible. The system becomes stressed, which many times negatively manifests itself in other areas, processes, and systems. With this in mind, when we view the lack of action on the part of an employee, we have to question ourselves as to why is it really occurring. For many people, it appears that they do not want to engage in any activity which they define as uninteresting, boring, dull, unfulfilling, or perceived as being "busy work." We address employee motivation and morale during our studies of human performance management and leadership because it appears that employees who do not like their job, specific position, or the company they work for, also do not enjoy the various tasks associated with or required of their current job or position. This of course many times causes an increase in the amount of and severity of the procrastination present or experienced. The increased use of "creative procrastination" by some team members today provides even more credence today for supervisors to attempt various corrective actions such as the "Premack Principle" when dealing with those who are habitual underperformers due to procrastination. Procrastination and lack of action can become so engrained in the employee's lifestyle and daily behavior, that it becomes part of their distinct personality traits. In such cases the employee will need help to change their patterns of negative behavior. At this point the "Premack Principle" may be of some use, before you seek additional professional assistance or engage in any sort of progressive discipline. The "Premack Principle" as just one method of possible corrective action involves a structured program of providing the subject with a few very easy and well-defined tasks to perform that can be easily measured by you as the supervisor and themselves as the subject requiring assistance. The idea is that when the employee has successfully completed a specific, assigned task, their supervisor will assign them another similar tasks, but somewhat more complicated or challenging. When that task is accomplished, the amount and complexity of the work assigned will continue to regularly increase. It has been proven that over a period of time, the employee's confidence levels, and work ethic will build and grow to a point where they can successfully complete their work without outside assistance and that they can in fact self-initiate the effort, activity, or action required of their position or job satisfactorily. They will hopefully now possess the long-term self-discipline and intestinal fortitude required to sustain their newfound improved performance into the future without constant assistance, support or supervision!

CHAPTER 13

THE CRITICAL NEED FOR LEADING THE ORGANIZATION!

Remember the cost of poor leadership and ineffective supervisory management practices will be measured, by you, your teams and the organization's failure to accomplish your mission.

The old cliché: "Every member of an organization is in fact a leader," is not just an age-old adage, but rather a critical belief that should be riveted into the mind of every member of the organization. From top leadership, with the blessing of corporate governance, to the most entry-level position, leadership sets the tone for the organization, including driving and ensuring the various work performance standards are achieved, including production, service, quality control, cutting waste/running lean, and risk mitigation. Leadership also ensures the constant assessment and evaluation of progress towards the implementation of the organization's strategic plan in total. Sometimes this involves initiating necessary changes and modifications to help ensure organizational success. All great leaders must remember that the first key to success is to make the right decision, then to communicate it thoroughly and continually, and finally to model the expected or desired behavior. In short, you must not only make good decisions, and "talk the talk," but also just as importantly, leaders at all levels must also "walk the talk". This provides the reinforcement of what actions and behaviors are required for the organization to be both efficient and effective! One last thought when discussing the criticality of leadership to organizational success. Organizations can no longer afford to become stagnant or complacent, much less tolerate internal resistance, competition, or conflict. Any potential issue must be identified and dealt with immediately and decisively, whether it is found to be passive resistance, office politics, internal risks, or any of a myriad of other typical risks possibly present. Always remember that leadership drives organizational success at every level, every day! No one is left out of this equation. Even the newest entry-level employee must have the desire to achieve success for themselves, the team, and the organization. They must possess some degree of self-discipline and be willing to work hard to improve themselves with the understanding that sacrifice is sometimes required if everyone on the team is to excel and experience success, including themselves. In short, leadership and team members' performance must be at their very best every day of the year!

Leadership accountability at every level, including organizational governance from legislative bodies, to privately elected boards, to appointed commissions, is critical to success. Unhealthy levels of internal competition are indeed a nemesis for many organizations today, but another very important issue for the leadership of any organization, is how to best align the organization's identified mission with their own vision for the future. The first phase of this process is just as mentioned previously, the board of governance for the organization decides where the organization is now in regards to achieving its mission, and then must also assess where the organization wants to be in the future. The governing body should then choose a leader who has the proven ability and drive to get them there. This is obviously much easier said than done. There are legislative bodies, elected officials, and even boards of directors who are not quite sure where their organization is right now, much less where it should be or wants to be in the future. In fact, research suggests that many CEOs should demand better direction from their own boards on what is the governing body's expectations and standards for performance, before they accept the position. In the very least they should be informed of these important pieces of information soon after taking control of the organization. The main reason for this is to prevent a board that does not give specific direction to the Chief Executive Officer (CEO) or Chief Operating Officer (COO), thus washing their hands of any responsibility in the future, for something possibly going wrong, and using the new leader as a very convenient scapegoat on which to rest any future blame. This blame game normally takes place with "plausible deniability" being claimed by those in higher levels of leadership in many large organizations, including government at times. If top leadership engages in some task or activity which is either wrong or goes astray, then the governing body can always fall back on, "we didn't know." That is many times what boards have been known to do. Being "asleep at the wheel" is not what shareholders pay board members to do. Governing bodies are supposed to research and study the organization and engage in meaningful dialogue with other board members and leadership to set direction and establish realistic yet challenging goals and objectives for the organization's performance. The board should be there in support of all organizational and leadership efforts and remain vigilant of all critical activities to ensure a set of checks and balances exists within the organization. This effort protects both the stockholder's and or constituent's interest and also helps safeguard the current and future viability of the organization.

Effectively engaging in problem solving, tactical vs. strategic planning, resource acquisition, talent management, decision making, and problem solving are but a few of the many challenges faced by supervisors, managers and leaders today. Many of these same issues and concerns have faced leaders throughout history. As with all learning, developing critical thinking skills through the review of past history can be quite enlightening. War often reveals the very best and very worst leadership traits in humans. For example, the Battle of Gettysburg was indeed critical to both the Union and Confederate forces during the American Civil War, and as such, provides the inquisitive learner with a unique opportunity to metaphorically study leadership theory, traits, characteristics, and application. Even the method of executing one's plans can still reveal complex challenges and additional perspectives to what appear many times to be simplistic situations and problems. General William Tecumseh Sherman recognized the need for this type of training at the United States Military Academy, when he developed the Military Staff Ride concept for his own staff officers in 1875. Today, the Military Staff Ride provides each participant with the opportunity to study the various principles of organizational behavior and leadership metaphorically, through the Civil War, and in particular the Battle of Gettysburg. Each participant should view the Staff Ride as a learning tool, designed to provide the learner with enhanced supervision, management, and leadership skills, in a generalized organizational setting. History provides all inquisitive learners with the opportunity to learn new and or additional theories, principles, and applications of effective leadership. These lessons fortunately come without the negative side effects and serious consequences that accompany poor decision making and leadership in the real world - including war of course. Learning to consider the humanistic aspects of our choices and decisions should in the very least become a by-product of this type of learning. The impact of our decisions as leaders on others both personally and professionally should be of paramount importance and the guiding light for each of us as we successfully lead our colleagues and organizations further into the 21st century.

CHAPTER 14

ASSESS LEADERSHIP PROGRESS AND EFFECTIVENESS FOR SUCCESS!

Always learn to develop your leadership knowledge, skills and abilities, and exemplify what true leadership is? We are all leaders at some level and to some degree.

Developing oneself as an effective leader is more complicated and challenging than it appears. The number of influences and variables affecting all of us as leaders is endless.

There are many different perspectives from which to study leadership: Some of the more prevalent are as follows:

- Traits
- Styles
- Theories
- Competencies
- Concepts
- Challenges
- Eras

- Strengths
- Approaches
- Orientation
- Models
- Values
- Philosophies
- Levels
- Principles

As one can see through reviewing the list above, the study of leadership can provide almost as many questions as it does answers. It is similar to choosing the right master's degree to pursue, the one that is most appropriate for yourself and simultaneously meets the needs of the organization you work for. The typical hallmark degree for those entering business has always been the Master of Business Administration (MBA); however, there appears to be a major movement taking place in the United States today towards a softer skillset, such as what can be found in the Master of Science (MS) or Master of Science in Management (MSM) degrees. As one might imagine, the MBA offers a greater focus on the harder business skill sets such as accounting, finance, statistics, and project management, whereas the MS and MSM degrees offer a greater emphasis on softer skills such as organizational behavior, decision making, change management, and effective leadership. Which degree to choose depends on one's perspective and needs, but it still lends credence to the question posed, which is, what is the best direction to head when trying to prepare oneself for a successful career in a leadership position? In short, we might be better off understanding and agreeing that a leader's level of self-awareness, emotional intelligence, and ability to strike the necessary balance of skills, knowledge and abilities (SKAs), based upon the situation they find themselves in, would be the most advantageous approach for success in today's organizations, particularly if in a leadership position.

With this in mind, we need to be able to recognize, understand, and effectively utilize various aspects of leadership as we push forward in our organizations. Whether it is the novice student of basic leadership theory, traits, and styles, or the veteran leader with years of experience simply trying to hone their approach, we must be able to use varying leadership concepts and principles to both our own and our team's advantage if we hope to be successful moving forward towards the accomplishment of our organization's mission!

Various leadership theories have abounded for decades, but let us look at some of the more popular and useful ones:

- Authentic Leadership Theory
- Servant Leadership Theory
- Leadership Exchange Theory
- Situational Leadership Theory
- Rational Leadership Theory
- Theory X and Y
- Contingency Leadership Theory
- Transformational vs. Transactional Leadership Theory

After reviewing each of these theories and after having worked in many supervisory management and leadership positions within a wide variety of organizations and populations, including both for-profit and non-profit, I believe combining Contingency Leadership Theory/ Situational Leadership Theory and Servant Leadership Theory are the most practical and easiest theories to use in any given situation. They work very well for a wide variety of leadership perspectives and are many times applicable in a wide variety of situations because they remain flexible as to the type of leadership style is best to use. In short,

Contingency Leadership Theory/Situational Leadership Theory entrusts you as the leader to be capable of switching leadership styles when needed based upon your own knowledge, skills, and abilities, recognizing the audience or population you are working with, and lastly understanding the type of situation you find yourself leading in. Contingency Leadership Theory truly makes the most sense for many of the very pragmatic situations one may find themselves in, yet it allows for the greatest flexibility in the leadership style used. This in turn leads to increased levels of leadership effectiveness. Because of the balancing of priorities which this theory allows, the leader is able to make major changes or shifts in style when needed, given the situation or circumstances faced. Remember, the greatest challenge of effective leadership is finding the balance between the needs of the situation present, and the people you are supervising, and your own ability as a leader.

After years of studying leadership in a wide variety of situations, and after having used Situational/Contingency and Servant based leadership many times in the past, I have found that Jim Kouzes' and Barry Posner's "5 Practices of Exemplary Leaders," which can also be found in their 2001 book and video *The Leadership Challenge*, is most helpful. After more than 30 years of research and work in the area of effective leadership, Jim Kouzes and Barry Posner present 5 of the most useful, yet basic tenets that every effective leader should use.

The "5 Practices of Exemplary Leaders" per *The Leadership Challenge* are:

- Model the way!
- Share in an agreed upon vision!
- Challenge the process!
- Empower your team!
- Say thank you and mean it!

After a review of this chapter, doesn't it seem that becoming an effective leader should be much easier to both obtain and sustain, and that more supervisors, managers and leaders across the United States, and the world today would be better off practicing these types of leadership theories and styles in their daily activities? Unfortunately, that doesn't' seem to be the case. I still find it amazing how many companies require both basic and advanced leadership training on the part of many of their leaders, yet when those same leaders return to their various positions in the organization, they implement very little, if any, of what they have learned. This is the difference between traditional leaders and the effective leaders of today and tomorrow – not who has the training, or even the position, but who has the real ability and, more importantly, the desire and courage to be a great leader. If you possess the skills, knowledge, and abilities to be a great leader, but do not utilize these same SKAs, then you are essentially a leadership liability, not an asset to the organization. I always ask new leaders if they have the courage to be a great leader? To more veteran leaders, I ask them what the cost-benefit of their current leadership style is to the organization? It could very well be that your current default leadership style is costing the organization in lost productivity and poor mission accomplishment.

CHAPTER 15

I'M A LEADER, NOW WHAT DO I DO?

There are many, many competencies required of great leaders today! Do you have what it takes? Ask yourself what qualities do you look for in a leader?

Before we can proceed any farther with our discussion on the importance of leadership to an organization's success or failure, we must first identify exactly what leadership is and what the typical requirements of effective leadership are today. First, let's define leadership. Leadership is "the ability to convince others to want to voluntarily follow you because of their respect for you and the overall credibility you possess as well as how they view your ability to successfully fulfill the requirements of the role of a leader". If one accepts the above definition of leadership, then we can proceed with identifying the typical competencies required of leaders.

According to the Federal Office of Personnel Management, some of the more prevalent leadership competencies today are as follows:

- Accountability and Ownership
- Analytical/Critical Thinking & Intellectual Capabilities (ability to reason)

- Challenging the Status Quo
- Collaboration/Cooperation/Integration
- Communication/Persuasion Creativity/Innovation
- Change Management
- Customer Centric
- Market Oriented
- Decisiveness
- Problem Solving and Prevention
- Leveraging Diversity
- Performance Based
- Results Driven
- Energy and Enthusiasm
- Finding/Managing and Developing Talent
- Possessing Global Perspective
- Integrity, Ethically based and Value-driven
- Interpersonal Skills
- Relationship Forming
- Strategic Thinking
- Vision
- Managing Information Systems and Technology

As one can see, the skills, knowledge, and abilities a leader should possess are quite daunting and not easily obtained or sustained. Please be reminded that leadership competencies are not the same as personality traits. Leadership "traits" have been studied for years, but the primary limitation of studying those who possess such traits, is the fact that many people can exhibit specific positive leadership traits, but still be bad leaders. In fact, I think most members of our country's employee workforce would agree that very few leaders today possess a majority of the various skillsets required to be a great leader, and even if they do, they only apply them when convenient or politically expedient for themselves. Many leaders and employees alike operate in such an irrational or emotionally charged manner, that many employees lose respect, trust, and confidence in their leaders and refuse to follow them anymore than absolutely necessary. In the following chapter, we will discuss this problem in more detail, because it is absolutely critical to the current and future success of individuals, the team, and the entire organization that employees want to follow their designated leaders!

Character or Competence? Which is more important to becoming and remaining a great leader? You decide. As just mentioned, your SKAs as a leader are critical to your success, if for no other reason than to gain credibility with others, whether those others be internal employees and colleagues, or external customers and stakeholders. Such consideration, however, reveals that the real question is: what is more critical to success as a leader – leadership competence, or leadership character? Which do you think is most critical to leadership effectiveness and why?

General Norman Schwarzkopf described it best to the cadets at West Point in 1993 while completing one of his final public speeches as a General in the United States Army. During that speech, General Schwarzkopf stated, "Leaders of the 21st century need two things to be a great leader: Character and Competence." Even though this is a somewhat oversimplified description, it is a very prophetic statement, because when all is said and done, he is right. Both the leaders of today and tomorrow must be committed enough and strong enough to make tough decisions when necessary and have the courage to sacrifice themselves for the betterment of the team and organization, all the while maintaining their ability to actually get the job done. Finding both of these qualities or characteristics in a leader today is quite difficult. In the book *Brave Decisions*, then Major Norman

Schwarzkopf displayed both of these qualities while a military officer in Vietnam. When faced with a politically charged decision by his commander, he made the right choice, to look out first for the safety and welfare of his soldiers, even though he knew his decision would be unfavorable with certain political powers and that his career might suffer as a result. Major Schwarzkopf made the right decision and had the character to take the hit for his troops, and in the end, he returned later to his colleagues even stronger and more respected than before. Unfortunately, few leaders today appear poised or willing to make the tough decisions and right decisions, for the right reasons, and are instead all too willing to place blame on others, if it is politically expedient for them to do so. We will discuss this problem further in our subsequent discussions on ethics and Corporate Social Responsibility.

Effective Leadership requires a very diverse skill set. Every time I see an advertisement for leadership training in our country today, it almost always emphasizes how to be a better one-on-one supervisor. I cannot dispute how true and necessary this is; however, I think if we stop our study of leadership with just that viewpoint, we have lost out on understanding that great leadership today is so much more than this! This perspective is not unusual though today, as even worldwide organizations like the International Association of Chiefs of Police (IACP) and others, have spent countless dollars and devoted years to developing and promoting new leadership training programs for current and future front-line supervisors in the field of policing. In official correspondence, the IACP's two current first line supervisor's training programs are called Leading Police Officers, or LPO for short and First Line Leadership or FLL for short. These programs are high quality, well-designed leadership development programs conceived for new supervisors, or even veteran supervisors who have lost their edge and need to in the late Stephen Covey's words "sharpen the saw." However, one of the major criticisms today of many first line supervisors' leadership development courses is that they concentrate too heavily on the humanistic and interpersonal side of leadership and not enough on the organization as a whole. This is why the study of organizational management and organizational leadership is so critical to supervisor, manager, and leader success! Supervisors, managers and leaders cannot possibly expect to be effective without understanding the intricacies and complexities of how the organization really works and its impact on them as a leader, individual employee or team.

After spending years working in a variety of career fields, I have become hypervigilant of just how much effort it takes to be a great leader, depending upon the work environment and type of organization you find yourself in. It goes beyond simply cultivating a successful personal relationship or being "nice" to your team members and others. The following skills sets and expectations will need to be addressed by every first line supervisor, mid-level manager, and executive, if they expect to be successful. One of the key points to being perceived as a great leader is one's credibility. As stated by Kouzes and Posner in previous chapters, credibility is the single most important quality required of great leaders because without it, followers won't follow, and you will have to resort to treating everyone like poorly performing subordinates and order them to execute the various tasks required of their job. As we all know, the results of this type of archaic, Authoritarian Leadership style, will net very few positive results for the long haul. Below you will see a number of other talents and skillsets which a truly great leader will need to possess and master if they hope to be successful for the long term and as they move up the corporate ladder. In fact, all that changes about these various leadership skillsets and competencies as your position in the organization changes, is the amount of time you spend utilizing each of them. Don't be naive or shortsighted by believing that if you work well with people, then that is all you have to worry about to be an effective leader!

Examples of various leadership skills, knowledge and abilities are:

- Ability to supervise interpersonally and develop followers.
- Utilize Organizational Management skills such as (planning, organizing, staffing, etc.)
- Possess the imagination, creativity, and drive to see the big picture, visualize the future, and set both current and future direction (think strategically, act tactically)
- Possess and understand organizational knowledge, history, past practices, and culture etc.
- Master the expected technical career field skills, knowledge, and abilities SKAs.

Just remember, if you are not good in your field of expertise, if you lack vision and the ability to inspire others, if you don't understand the organization and how it really works, don't possess basic management skills such as delegating, scheduling, organizing, and assessing, and are unable to inspire others and develop interpersonal and professional relationships with your fellow teams members, you will immediately lose your credibility, effectiveness, and ability to lead others both inside and outside the organization. Great leaders possess all of the above-described leadership competencies and SKAs to varying degrees and know how to balance them accordingly based off the current situation or need!

CHAPTER 16

DEVELOP FOLLOWERSHIP, NOT SUBORDINATESHIP!

*Great leaders recognize and develop followers, not subordinates, and realize the criticality of developing their team member's **Trust** to their success.*

More often than not it seems we spend countless hours in the classroom presenting or discussing material on leadership and why we need to be better leaders, yet at the end of day no one ever explains or shows their audience how to actually do it! How do I accomplish what I just spent all of this time talking about doing? In a very simplified formula, we can start to get a handle on how to actually work on becoming better leaders and help those we work with become better followers. The leader-follower relationship can be very complex and dynamic, and also both synergistic and satisfying for each party if approached from the right perspective. We must first recognize, just as Kelley did in *The Power of Followership*, that there are very distinct followership styles, just as there are very specific leadership styles. According to his model, you could be considered a "passive" or "active" follower or a "dependent" or "independent" follower. Regardless of your constituent's style of following, you as a formal leader within the organization need to recognize the various types and styles of followers and get to know each style better if you ever hope to effectively harness all the hard work, energy, and talent that employees bring to you, the team and the organization.

We desperately need to become better leaders in our organizations, which will in turn help those we are responsible for to want to voluntarily follow us, not because they are our subordinates, but because they truly want to. One final, but critical thought to remember when approaching the concept of leadership vs. followership, is to remember to make good decisions, effectively communicate those decisions to all interested parties and to finally model the expected or appropriate behavior. These three key factors in developing followers must be supported regularly by the other critical competencies and skill sets required of great leaders, including effective management skills, technical skills, career skills, and organizational knowledge. Without a balance of all of these leadership skills, you will neither possess, nor display the credibility and competence required to maintain loyal and dedicated followers. Your potential followers will most assuredly recognize a "hollow shirt" during their interactions with you, if you don't live up to and follow the followership formula/ model presented here.

The Leader-Follower Trust Building model:

A GOOD DECISION, COMMUNICATED WELL & EFFECTIVELY MODELED
▼

Builds *Credibility and Confidence*
▼

Which fosters a positive *Personal* and *Professional Relationship*,
▼

Team members realize *their Values and Character align with yours*
▼

So fellow team members learn to *Respect You* and *Trust you*,
▼

and if they Trust you, they will Follow You!
▼

To support this viewpoint, let's look at Kouzes' and Posner's article *Credibility: What Followers Expect*. After surveying over 75,000 people worldwide, the authors were able to identify four critical characteristics of great leaders. Those characteristics were: honest, forward-thinking, inspirational, and competent. To both develop and maintain the leader-follower relationship, you must as the model reveals build the relationship via making good decisions, effectively communicating those decisions, and finally by displaying the appropriate behavior expected of someone in a leadership position in a similar situation. One should then continue to support the leader-follower relationship and the trust that has been developed, with high levels of character and competence in all leadership endeavors engaged in both personally and professionally. Subscribing to the Leader-Follower Trust Building model on a daily basis will undoubtedly help build and sustain the critical trust required for being an effective leader. Once your credibility comes into question, you will lose your constituents' and followers' confidence, respect and most of all trust. Once the positive leader-follower relationship has been broken, only bad things can happen from that point forward for all parties involved!

CHAPTER 17

MAKE GOOD DECISIONS THAT MAKE SENSE?

Make sure you don't jump to conclusions too quickly and always make sure your decisions make sense if you expect others to follow you.

Great leadership requires so many of the traits and competencies presented in earlier chapters, but as stated the first test of a leader's real worth to the organization is their ability to make good decisions and either prevent or solve problems. Making good choices as we teach our children precipitates good outcomes, either immediately or in the future. There are in fact two general types of decisions to be made in the world of work: those which are proactive in nature and are necessary for the execution of some part of the strategic plan, and second, the decisions which are reactionary in nature and are required to address some problem, question, concern, or issue which has already arisen. Of course, the reactionary piece to this puzzle can also be something as simple as making an adjustment in performance or as complex as changing an activity which is not currently in alignment with the organization's overall mission. Leaders must be able to master effective decision-making in both proactive and reactive situations; if not, they will lose all credibility with their team, and quite possibly lose their own self-confidence in making decisions as well. A leader or team member should be capable of handling a situation with either the innate and or learned ability required to make the right choice and continue to build a solid foundation for great leadership and performance.

We must remember that one of the most critical situations we face as leaders is the making of decisions, particularly when in the face of unforeseen problems or variables. Our employees, colleagues, supervisors, and other stakeholders are watching how we make critical decisions that affect them and the organization and ultimately how positive or negative the results are. We gain confidence, respect, credibility, and momentum for the next decision we have to make when we succeed in learning from our current and past decisions and performance. Both positive and negative outcomes alike help build our intuition and wisdom for making future decisions. We can draw on this experience for the next situation we face as either an employee or leader. Some say that making decisions is kind of like leadership – you are either born with the ability or not. I, and almost every other leadership expert in the country, will tell you yes, there are those who have a natural propensity for becoming leaders and making good decisions, but to a greater extent we are all a product of our environment, training, education, and experience. In this light, making good decisions can be credited in some cases to innate ability, but more often than not it stems from multiple variables and attributes, including the decision analysis process, where we try to use a rational decision-making model, and not our personal intuition to make the right decision. Even if we have great inter-personal skills and form effective relationships with others, but we continually make poor decisions and choices, our credibility will still become questioned and tarnished, with no one, not even those who "like us" wanting to follow us.

Some of the more popular decision-making models and tools available today are:

- Force Field Analysis
- Decision Tree
- Critical Path Analysis
- Nominal Group Technique
- Fault Tree

These are just a few of the many possible Rational Decision-Making models available today. We should also recognize the similarities between the typical problem-solving models and decision-making models. They are not just related to one another but are in fact so dependent on one another that they are many times interdependent. There is one incredibly important variable to take into consideration when making good decisions, and that is to make sure you possess good information with which to base your decisions. Making the right decisions is doomed from the start if you try to do so without the appropriate data, information, and/or intelligence required.

The typical steps to effective decision-making and problem-solving can be seen here:

- Correctly identify the true issue to be addressed (the decision or problem)
- Identify a process, procedure, and methodology for solving the issue at hand!
- Collect, compile, and collate the data to be presented as usable information!
- Analyze the information and generate usable business intelligence!
- Generate viable alternatives and solutions!
- Implement the best solution or course of action!

- Assess and modify where required!
- Debrief the entire process and learn for future situations and applications!

As we can see, the problem-solving model looks very much like the decision-making model, which in turn looks very much like the process for conducting research. In this vein we can recognize both the convergence and interrelatedness of conducting thorough research and using that research (data, information, and intelligence) in the daily decision-making models that we utilize in our problem-solving processes. My hope is that upon further study, we will all realize that we should never make decisions in a vacuum, but rather be open-minded and understanding the input presented from the "other side." The number of variables which exist in making decisions and/or solving problems today is far too complex for just one person to assume they can handle it alone using just their intuition. While intuition may work in certain cases, one cannot rely on that forever, particularly when employees and supervisors want to see the rationale behind the decisions you are making. See below for the why we need to know how to facilitate effective decision making and take the appropriate action to address the current situation.

Measure, assess and evaluate the progress made towards one of the following:

- Implementing the decision (proactive)
- Solving the problem (reactive)
- Addressing the issue or concern (reactive)
- Answering the question (reactive)
- Affecting the change (proactive or reactive - depending)
- Initiating a new idea (proactive)
- Make the required adjustments (reactive)

Out of all that we have discussed in regards to making good decisions, there is one last point we need to mention, particularly when solving problems, and that is that any decisions made need to be completed as expediently as possible, since most issues in life and at work are time sensitive. Remember, one of the positive traits everyone expects from you as a leader is to be decisive and timely. If you do not meet the need for timeliness, the problem may not go away on its own as you may have hoped, but could in fact blossom into a crisis, which if addressed in a timely manner could have possibly been avoided or at least minimized!

I continually see many authors preaching the need for being proactive and taking action. However, my concern is that I see these same authors who preach constant proactivity, state that being reactive is always a negative attribute, when in reality many of them are afraid to admit that occasional adjustments will be needed to either their strategic and or tactical plans, as an appropriate response to some type of feedback they have received. I believe it is naïve to continually believe and teach that an organization can implement a strategic plan in this ever changing and incredibly complicated world we function in without making necessary adjustments when required, sometimes even on a daily basis. The number of independent and dependent variables present at work today is endless and no one could ever anticipate every possible course of action required of implementing an entire strategic plan or operating a large organization. In fact, if I did not see an organization making regular and sometimes substantial changes to their original plans and responding to outside influences when needed, I would worry tremendously about the organization's future viability. The entire reason for assessing and evaluating progress is to make the necessary adjustments when required for success. Those organizations, who do not think they need to make tactical adjustments on a regular basis, probably have leadership who are either extremely lethargic or otherwise "asleep at the wheel." That type of complacency will likely threaten or negatively impact either your market share or total viability as an organization. We should not allow "mission creep" to lead us astray from our originally identified goals, objectives, and vision, but at the same time we should not drive with our eyes closed either, failing to recognize when adjustments to our plans or activities is required. Great organizations recognize opportunities when they arise and therefore make the right decisions and change their direction when needed!

CHAPTER 18

COMMUNICATE EFFECTIVELY BOTH INTERNALLY AND EXTERNALLY!

Communicate continually where the organization has been, is currently, and where it is going! People are starved for information and want to know; remember they have a very vested interest in what is going on and how it affects them, both personally and professionally!

Effective interpersonal communications: it always sounds like the typical cliché when we discuss the importance of successfully operating an organization, but it is nevertheless true. Effective interpersonal communications are critical to the operations of every organization. Without effective communication we cannot accomplish any of the many tasks that we must achieve if we ever hope to successfully fulfill the mission of the organization. It is true – communication at every level is the "glue" that holds the system together and ensures things function as they should. Developing and implementing a successful strategic plan within the organization, comes down to communicating with everyone involved, all in an effort to "get all of the players on the same page." Engaging in positive interpersonal communications is one of the three key ingredients to true leadership and convincing your fellow team members to follow you because they want to, not because they have to.

As stated in chapter 17, the first key ingredient in building credibility and trust, is to make a good decision. This goes without saying that this competency is a must for any leader to gain and sustain everyone's trust. Leaders are expected to be able to make good decisions. The second key ingredient however is effective interpersonal communications. Leaders are again expected to communicate well with everyone around them and to keep everyone apprised of both the good and bad. As stated, the typical team member is starved for information, particularly when it affects them! The third ingredient is to model the expected behavior and to remain professional at all times. In a very real sense this is also a form of communication. When you engage in any type of behavior, particularly as a supervisor, manager, or leader in an organization, you send a real and powerful message to others as to what your expectations are, and what the standards of performance are within the organization. You can even help to change or solidify your corporate culture by revealing to others what your beliefs, morals, and values are as a leader within the organization. I think it is easy to recognize how incredibly important effective interpersonal communication is to the efficient operation of an organization.

For any leader to be able to effectively use their supervisory management and leadership skills and abilities, they must first have mastered the art and science of communication. As stated, communication is the "glue" that allows all human interactions to take place successfully. Without effective interpersonal communication we cannot relay the information, feelings, and direction we intended, as we attempt to influence others to want to follow us. Whether it is internal, external, formal or informal, good communications is absolutely critical to effective leadership. Communication in the case of supervisory management and leadership is all about sending an accurate message both verbally and visually and ensuring that the receiver interprets the proper message – the one you intended. This is a critical area for every leader to remember, because so many problems in our workplaces today involve misinterpretations, misunderstandings, or incorrect assumptions, all of which are forms of miscommunications or a lack of communications! Human beings are emotional creatures, and organizations are very complex entities. Organizations are hard enough to keep running smoothly, even without throwing ineffective interpersonal communications in on top of that. Once the misinformation or miscommunication has transpired, the damage is done, and now the leader and everyone involved must spend an inordinate amount of time and energy to try to correct and or address the situation left behind.

Communications is not only critical to the successful completion of daily operational and administrative tasks, but also to the success of the strategic management and operational management processes. For instance, if a leader does not effectively communicate the organization's current and future direction, how then will employees know what action or behavior they should be engaging in, to help further the organization's agreed upon vision. With this, you might recognize the statement "agreed upon." The vision of every leader and the impact they have on the organization's direction must be communicated to them effectively, so that it can be understood, accepted and become a "shared vision" for everyone.

Whether it is communicating the daily tasks that need to be accomplished tactically, or communicating the long-range strategic direction of the organization, effective interpersonal communication must be engaged in on a continual basis if we are to be successful in getting "our message" across to all of our many stakeholders. It is true – communications are the lynch pin and glue that holds the entire system together and allows a leader to drive an organization towards its ultimate goal of high performance and success!

We should all endeavor to remember what George Bernard Shaw said: "The single biggest problem with communication is the illusion that it has taken place." So, with that, always try to err on the side of over-communication. Your supervisors, peers, and subordinates will tell you when you are communicating too much. Better that, than having many, many critical items "falling between the cracks", because team members assumed the message had been conveyed and interpreted correctly. Communications is both the key to the successful implementation of the strategic plan and for setting the correct direction for the organization's future! How can you possibly "manage the process" towards successfully accomplishing the organization's mission and vision if you cannot or will not communicate effectively with others?

CHAPTER 19

MODEL THE APPROPRIATE AND EXPECTED BEHAVIOR!

Model the expected behavior and standards of performance. Lead the way by showing everyone how to do it right, the first time!

Leadership training exists all over the country in so many shapes and forms, from OJT to advanced graduate level college courses. Despite this, one thing no one really ever takes the time to explain is how leadership actually works in "the field" or real world. This presents a huge problem, because countless thousands of people attend various types of leadership training in the United States every day, and still return to their jobs with no knowledge as to how to actually apply what they have just learned to the real-world situations they face daily. Mechanically, how does leadership actually work? In short there are certain steps attributed to every leadership process.

The actual leadership process is shown sequentially below:

- Faced with a possible or potential leadership situation or issue (initiate, decide, or solve)
- Decide whether or not to take action or get involved!

- Conduct research and develop alternative solutions or options!
- Decide on the appropriate course of action!
- Communicate that decision to all stakeholders!
- Role model the appropriate behavior for all stakeholders to see by successfully implementing the decision.
- Assess the impact of your decision and learn from it for future reference.

The leadership process is very much like the strategic planning process in that it has specific parts and steps that make it successful. At the same time, it is also sequential, requiring every step to be taken in the correct order or you risk making the wrong decision and hurting your credibility as a leader. When it really comes down to it, success isn't about leadership versus management so much as it is more about merging various supervisory, management, and leadership skills, knowledge and abilities into a contingency style of leading, again based upon your ability as a leader, the situation you face, and the audience you are leading. The result is your personal and professional method of blending everything you have learned into a style of leadership that suits both the situation you find yourself leading in and the population or audience you find yourself leading at the time. If this sounds familiar, it should, because this is the same cross of Situational Leadership Theory and the Contingency Leadership Theory discussed earlier.

The key to success as a leader is of course, finding the right mix and balance of the various skills, knowledge, and abilities required in any given situation and then blending them into a flexible and appropriate method of leading for the circumstances present. Remember, leading typically means taking the initiative and necessary action to make complex decisions, solve unexpected problems, or make necessary adjustments to assist in the implementation of the strategic plan. With this in mind, we have to model the expected or appropriate behavior of a professional, if we can ever hope to be a well-balanced and successful leader. Remember, if we can make good decisions and choices, for both ourselves and our teams, and in fact communicate those decisions well, and then model the expected behavior by implementing those decisions effectively, then we can continue to grow our followers trust in us. It is truly up to us to help our subordinates and fellow team members develop into successful followers. Team members who trust us and depend on us every day to be effective and successful leaders expect us to act and behave in a responsible and professional manner no matter what type of situation is faced. To the extent that our direct reports and fellow team members develop and grow into followers, who are voluntarily willing to allow us the privilege of supervising, managing, and leading them farther into the 21st century, many times depends solely on us choosing and using the right leadership style, and using it to assist us in making good decisions, communicating those decisions well and acting in a professional manner by modeling the expected or appropriate behavior!

CHAPTER 20

GREAT LEADERSHIP AND SITUATIONAL PERFORMANCE REQUIRE DEVELOPING HIGH LEVELS OF SELF-AWARENESS, SOCIAL- AWARENESS AND SELF-MANAGEMENT!

Effective situational performance requires you to strive to learn about yourself, both your strengths and weaknesses, and ask what others see in you, that you cannot?

S elf-awareness is critical to leading others. As we know, leaders can only be great if they can first effectively lead themselves. Followers will never become more than subordinates if they fail to develop respect, trust, and confidence in their leaders. As Daniel Goleman states in his first book, *Emotional Intelligence*, self-awareness is absolutely critical for one to become effective and successful as a leader today. Knowing one's areas of expertise and natural skills and interest, versus just their own basic personality traits, allows one to be a more effective leader. Great leaders understand the limitations of their own skills, knowledge, and abilities. The same holds true for successful followers. Just as importantly, by recognizing both their personal and professional limitations, leaders and followers alike can then take the steps necessary to remain effective in spite of any such challenges they might face. One cannot possibly accentuate their natural attributes and address their negative traits if they are not even aware of them or fail to recognize their existence. It has always been said that a successful leader does not have to possess all of the skillsets required for success in a specific job or position, but simply be aware of their own limitations, and locate others who can effectively address those various areas where they as leaders are either limited or challenged.

Leadership isn't always about having the requisite skills, knowledge, and ability, but rather an open-mindedness and willingness to seek out others who might be able to assist them in being an effective leader in a wide variety of situations. For those people who do not understand where their own weaknesses and needs for possible change are, the term "Johari Window" has been coined. It is said that this window is the window to your soul. The "Johari Window" is a look into the innate traits and characteristics that make you who you are. It is a composite of your genetics, formative years, life experiences, education, and training, ultimately culminating in who you are as a person. One's values, principles, character traits etc. obviously transfer over to how one acts outwardly, both personally and professionally. If your level of Self-Awareness and the "Johari Window" are this important to your effectiveness as a person and leader, the next obvious goal should be, how to both identify and determine to what degree you possess any positive or negative personality and character traits that affect your ability to lead. In short, how do you address the items you identified during your assessment of your own self-awareness?

Some of the easiest methods to help build self-awareness are the following:

- Engage in various personality trait tests, such as the Myers-Brigg, DISC Personality profile, and Minnesota Multi-Phasic Personality Inventory
- Engage in various IQ tests, including the traditional Stanford Binet, etc.
- Engage in a wide variety of self-assessments.
- Anonymously survey others
- Request a 360-degree evaluation by your subordinates.
- Complete an interview by a licensed psychologist who focuses on Industrial Psychology

The key to getting to know oneself is to not only experience as much as possible in life, but to also take the time to look inward and perform some degree of self-reflection and introspection on a regular basis. One can certainly learn valuable lessons in life from every experience, whether it be personal or professional. Leadership is relational, and relationships are all about people – the people you are leading and also the effect of your personal style as a leader on others. The late Dr. Massey stated that the only way to get a person to really change their viewpoint in life is for them to experience some major life-changing event. I don't necessarily agree with this. I believe that over a period of time, a person can slowly experience the same type of realization, or revelation about who they are, what they stand for, and why they are here. As Rick Warren states in a *Purpose Driven Life*, each of us has to know what it is we stand for and why we are here; in short, what is our purpose in life?

There are many different methods people can use to change their various characteristics. For example, one can intentionally engage in and experiment with new thought processes and behaviors, which will possibly expose them to a wide variety of currently unrealized thoughts, ideas and viewpoints. Intentionally taking yourself out of your "comfort zone" can be a great learning experience for anyone, but it is particularly beneficial for those in leadership positions. So many people spend a great deal of time working towards their desired level of "psychological comfort", that they never learn anything new or enlightening about themselves or their own abilities. Another method which can be used to change oneself is to simply let nature take its course, using wisdom and intuition, which as we all know is the gradually accumulated knowledge and common sense one obtains as they experience life. There are additional methods and strategies for changing oneself, but as you can see, being narrow-minded or close-minded throughout one's personal and professional life will most definitely have a negative impact on your success at work and as a leader. Never be too proud to admit when you are ignorant of a topic, even if that topic is yourself. The old adage "ignorance is bliss" or "that's just the way they are" are ridiculous statements; it may assist some in feeling more comfortable about themselves, but if that is your dominant viewpoint towards yourself and your surrounding environment, then being in a leadership position is probably not right for you anyhow!

So, if you are in fact up to the challenges of leadership and assisting others in achieving their highest possible potential, or simply want to enhance your own individual performance, you should be asking the obvious question, how can I do all of this? The following model developed by the author is a composite of the very best and most useful leadership development theories, performance management techniques and trust building/followership activities available today, all combined into one comprehensive model capable of assisting you in achieving all of the goals you should want to as a high performing member or leader in an organization!

The Warren Situational Performance Model (SPM)

Step 1 – Recognize the situation as a **Leadership requirement or opportunity**

Step 2 – Analyze the **Situation**

Step 3 – Analyze the **Audience** or population you are interacting with

Step 4 – Assess your own **Skills, Knowledge, Ability** & experience level in this type of situation

Step 5 – Select the correct **Leadership Style** to engage with

Step 6 – Make the appropriate **Decision** on how to best engage as a leader

Step 7 – Effectively **Communicate** the decision you made

Step 8 – Model the appropriate **Behavior** or action

Step 9 – **Assess** your progress and modify your decision, actions or style if needed

Step 10 – **Debrief** yourself and your performance and **Learn** for future use

As can be seen from reviewing the model above, there are several different, but critical components to ensuring you achieve the results you desire as you attempt to become either a high performing leader, or team member in an organization.

The principles the Warren Situational Performance Model is predicated upon.

1. The Warren Followership Formula for developing Trust.
2. Emotional Intelligence theory including Self-awareness, Social-awareness and Self-management.

3. <u>Situational and Contingency Leadership</u> theory and selecting the correct <u>Leadership Style</u> for the situation faced.

4. Criticality of effective <u>decision making, interpersonal communication skills, and ensuring your actions always exuberate a high degree of professionalism</u> in building credibility and trust.

5. Becoming a <u>life-long learner,</u> and assisting in <u>building a learning organization</u>

The above list of both critical principles and components to the Warren **Situational Performance Model (SPM)** reveals a wide variety of interdisciplinary and interrelated fields of study when it comes to leadership and human performance enhancement. The real key to the model's effectiveness is predicated upon the team member or leader being able to select the correct leadership style to use for the situation they are currently faced with as shown in step 5 of the **Situational Performance Model (SPM)**. Using their skills, knowledge and ability in relation to their own Self-awareness, Social-awareness and Self-management will assist them exponentially in identifying and using the correct leadership style as they push forward through the three critical steps of the **Situational Performance Model** – 1) Make a good decision, 2) Communicate that decision effectively and of course 3) Model the expected or appropriate behavior! However, as step 5 of the model reveals, choosing the correct leadership style based upon your own ability, the audience or population you are leading and the type of situation you find yourself in is critical to your success as a team member or leader. The final question then becomes when using this model is what are my choices for leadership styles? There are many different types of leadership styles depending largely on which research, text or author you are consulting. However, several of the most common and in some cases the most effective are in list form below.

The most common leadership styles in use today:

Autocratic – Makes all of the decisions in a vacuum.

Bureaucratic – Requires strict adherence to following the policies, procedures and rules.

Democratic – Commonly referred to as "participative" and looks for consensus when possible.

Laissez-Faire – Typically "hands off" and is many times disengaged.

Visionary – Drives progress towards goals, particularly during periods of change.

Pacesetter – Fast paced and sets standards of performance to motivate others.

Coaching – Recognizes team members' strengths and weaknesses and mentors them.

Servant – A "people first" mind set prevails, thus building trust and commitment to the team and the organization's mission and vision.

It is incredibly important for both your current and future performance and success that you choose the right leadership style with which to engage others with. Every internal team member and external stakeholder responds differently to various leadership styles and in different types of situations. Thus, the reason why the **Situational Performance Model** is so effective, because it is extremely flexible and nimble if the person using it possesses a high degree of situational awareness, social awareness and self-awareness/ management skills. As with all theories, principles, styles and skills sets, the **Situational Performance Model** is only as effective as the person using it. They must be both open-minded enough and willing enough to realize that the leadership style they use every day during their interactions with others both internally and externally can have a tremendously positive or negative effect on their success! Do you use a default style every day regardless of the situation, or are you willing to work towards becoming a more effective team member and leader by selecting the right leadership style for the type of situation you face? The real indicator of success is to ultimately accomplish our missions and attain our visions as individuals, teams, and organizations! The Warren **Situational Performance Model (SPM)** is both a composite and comprehensive leadership and situational performance model and training program designed to help us do just that!

CHAPTER 21

GREAT LEADERS REMOVE BARRIERS TO SUCCESS!

Develop successful work structures and workflows through designing effective processes and systems, and continually manage those processes removing anything that might be considered a barrier to success!

One of a leader's most important roles in an organization is to not only set direction and lead everyone's efforts towards accomplishing the goals and objectives that have been established and agreed upon, but to also eliminate any and all barriers to success which could arise within the organization. Employees and lower-level supervisors in many organizations regularly complain that they want to work hard and perform at higher levels, but that the processes and systems currently in place prohibit them from doing so. There appears to be some validity to this conclusion in many organizations today. Many large organizations are so complex that various frustrations and barriers occur as a result of simple day-to-day operations. The reality is that in some places employees wonder if some processes and systems were almost purposely designed to be a hindrance to employees' performance. This problem can sometimes manifest itself in elevated levels of either individual or team frustrations, due to the implementation of too many policies, procedures and processes, not having enough of them, having those which are not clear, or those which no one has been properly trained for or practiced enough. Many times, there are too many steps required in internal processes, many of which don't make sense to the employee anyhow, because no one ever took the time to explain the who, what, when, where, why, and how of the policy, procedure or process, and why it is so important to the system functioning properly.

As stated, one of the most serious negative by-products of large organizations is that the many policies, procedures, and processes required to make things operate smoothly, can have the exact opposite intended effect. Unfortunately, this phenomenon is often exacerbated by supervisors, managers, and leaders who place too much importance on control instead of motivating their employee workforce's performance. Frustration levels can elevate significantly when employees are placed in a work environment with too much emphasis on control, and which places them under the auspices of supervisors, managers, and leaders who philosophically or pragmatically support micromanagement. This can quickly get out of control in a setting where employees are constantly bombarded with such "red tape" and other barriers to success. In short, it is the leader's responsibility to identify and eliminate any overt or covert barriers affecting the organization's overall success. Even more importantly, they must not become one of those barriers themselves, by becoming too unchanging, disengaged, micromanaging, controlling, or obsessive-compulsive with regard to the organization's daily administration and operations. In the end, leadership is all about balancing your ability to lead within the confines of the organization's strategic plan and finding ways to eliminate anything that might stand in the way of the organization's success! Unfortunately, one of the most common barriers to success today exist internally, where poor or inept leadership prevails within the organization itself.

So then, what are we to do when we have leaders who don't lead, managers who don't manage, and supervisors who don't supervise? If your organization suffers from this issue, I truly feel for you. The shame of it is that in America today many of us, as members of organizations both large and small, suffer from this phenomenon to differing degrees. There seems to be no greater frustration on the part of both employees and leaders themselves, than having colleagues who refuse to do their job. The most important question to answer here is how to become a high performing organization when your leadership fails to lead, manage, or otherwise supervise its employees effectively. At some point even great employees will begin to become complacent regarding their performance if they feel that it doesn't make a difference, or that their superiors aren't doing their job effectively or carrying their fair share of the workload too. It is ironic that a recent survey of corporate CEOs revealed that one of their greatest frustrations was with employees and team members who were not successfully executing their assigned tasks. What about supervisors who don't execute their duties and responsibilities successfully? Such poor attitudes and lack of a work ethic, whether possessed by employees or leadership, runs counter to the implementation of the organization's strategic plan and will most assuredly keep the organization from successfully achieving its mission and attaining its vision!

Knowing this we must ask ourselves why some employees don't perform well and, more importantly, why some of our leadership also fails to perform up to expectations? There are many possible answers to these questions: it could result from a bypassed promotion, personality conflict with the boss or another colleague, or it may have arisen after failed attempts to gain additional training, the possible causes are almost endless. Unfortunately, there are many reasons why leaders who don't lead still get promoted to supervisory positions; from riding one's coattails to waiting others out and just letting nature take its course, however, the end result is the same for all, poor performance by team members due to increased levels of frustration with leadership. Once elevated to their new position the organization may find that they now have a person in a supervisory position with limited leadership skills, knowledge, or ability. When newly appointed and even veteran leaders alike do not have the ability or even desire to supervise, manage, or lead, their organizations can find themselves in real trouble.

In such instances where leaders either can't or won't lead, what happens? All leadership experts will attest to the negatives that arise in organizations that possess poor leadership. Leadership is such a critical requirement for success today, that without great or at least effective leadership, you can easily "crash and burn" as a team or even entire organization!

Let's take a chronological look at what negative consequences could arise with the failure of leadership and the "crashing" of an organization:

- Have a weak or poorly identified mission.
- Lack of commitment by political jurisdiction or top corporate governance.
- Choosing a top leader with the wrong skill set or wrong personality type for the job.
- The top leader's lack of vision, drive, commitment, technical skills, ethics, etc.
- Leadership don't know how to or refuse to commit to the development of a strategic plan.
- A lack of "buy-in" and/or commitment by both employees and other stakeholders.
- Weak development of all of the policies, procedures, and processes required.
- Failure to effectively implement the strategic plan throughout the organization.

- Employees and supervisors faced with a poorly developed plan and without the resources needed to execute the various strategies and tasks associated with the same.

- Top leadership finally recognizing the poor performance demand compliance.

- Micromanaging and utilizing a stricter style of leadership supporting a punitive work environment for everyone.

- Leadership attempts to shift blame for poor performance, resulting in rampant "Scape-goating."

- Plummeting morale and motivation to comply with management's demands (causing some employees to engage in passive resistance and others to deliberately sabotage the organization).

- Decreases in the big five occur: Productivity, Customer Service, Quality Control, Running Lean and Cutting Waste, and Risk Mitigation.

- All internal and external stakeholders become frustrated and disengaged.

- Bad press and loss of reputation results in loss of business (breaking of contracts and commitments, and the loss of new sales).

- Lack of sales is felt immediately (inventory increases, employees are laid off and the bottom line is in trouble).

- Profits decrease dramatically and cash flow can fall to dangerously low levels.

- Analyst, outside regulators, auditors, and stockholders become concerned and react.

- Stock values drop immediately, which results in major profit-sharing losses.

- Morale drops further and key employees, supervisors, technicians, specialists, etc., leave.

- Further cost cutting measures are implemented – firings, layoffs, no OT, etc.
- Operating budgets are stripped, and certain organizational functions are either merged with others, closed altogether, or are outsourced.
- Further cost cutting measures hurt morale even more as the "little guy takes the hit."
- With the future in question internal stress skyrockets while morale continues to plummet.
- Some supervisors and employees start intense competition with one another while "fighting" for the remaining jobs.
- Higher rates of attrition, grievances, and even lawsuits are experienced.
- Inept leadership, supervisors, and managers are now in a self-preservation/survival mode.
- Organization enters a complete, uncorrectable "downward spiral."
- Organization in complete crisis management and grasping for solutions to stop their inevitable failure.
- Filing of Chapter 11, looking for a buyer, merger, complete bankruptcy, etc., all possible at this point towards the end of the organization's life expectancy!

As one can see, once poor or inept leadership takes hold in an organization, many possible negative conditions can abound very quickly. If this process continues without some type of serious intervention, such as adding or repositioning new leadership, many of the steps presented above will undoubtedly occur as the problem becomes more pervasive and systemic. These conditions, including the circumstances surrounding the companies who fell off the original Fortune 500 list, are all too perfect examples of what happens when poor leadership prevails! Remember, leadership drives success, but it can also become a barrier to success and even drive failure!

SECTION 6

Sustaining and Growing High Performance and Success!

CHAPTER 22

ALWAYS ENSURE THAT ETHICS DRIVE THE ORGANZIATION AND ALL OF ITS MEMBERS!

Identify and communicate to everyone individual, team and corporate values, and enforce ethical standards to build a strong and viable organization, capable of mitigating and managing risks.

I would like to believe that we do not really need to include this chapter, but when we discuss leadership today, it is important to discuss an individual's behavior in regards to ethics, as well as an organization's ethics and culture. I have heard people state that their behavior was ethical because it wasn't prohibited by law. Understanding ethics and ethical behavior involves so much more than just strictly following the law.

We will start with a discussion of manners, etiquette, norms, values, and statutory law (both civil and criminal). As you can see, this abbreviated, yet sequential list of ethical terminology almost appears to emulate the chronology of progressive discipline, from the least serious, to the most serious transgressions. A person's behavior can range from bad manners and etiquette, all the way up to the point of breaking a statutory law, where they may be held criminally and civilly responsible for their behavior and actions. We must also not forget that the failure to act when one should, can also constitute unethical or illegal behavior. Rather than cover every eventuality, let's look at what is really critical for an organization when it comes to ensuring ethical behavior and actions within the workplace. A strong sense of ethics and corporate social responsibility starts with great leadership driving this attitude and position. This starts with taking the time to hire the right people, enforcing the organization's rules and regulations on a daily basis, and solidifying the organization's ethical culture whenever and wherever possible. Leadership has to establish the ethical tone of the entire organization by setting the standards of conduct for every person at every level. You might wonder how a leader is supposed to control the behavior of so many people at one time. The answer is that it has to be a comprehensive effort, starting at the very top with corporate governance, transferring down to executive level leadership, and then permeating down through all levels of management, supervision, and personnel, regardless of your job, position or rank!

The critical keys and steps to developing an ethical culture are presented below:

- Corporate governance establishes the vision of the organization, part of which includes how you expect to fulfill the organization's mission in an ethical manner.
- Transferring that expectation for ethical behavior to the members of the organization by hiring a CEO who has a reputation for introducing, living, and enforcing ethical behavior.
- The CEO and their top leadership team not only communicate their expectation for ethical behavior to everyone and at every

level throughout the organization, but model that behavior through each and every one of their decisions and actions, both tactically and strategically.

- The organization, under the direction of the CEO, establishes a set of core values, a code of conduct, (oath of office if applicable), and a set of written rules and regulations, supported by appropriate policy, all of which are well communicated both verbally and in writing to all stakeholders, both internally and externally.

- HR and all facets of talent management are directed to recruit and hire only those persons who are explicitly ethical. (The FBI for example has a recruitment adage "past performance equals future performance"). Those who possess past inappropriate behavior or who, through established selection processes and testing, may be deemed a divertible risk to the organization are eliminated from consideration for employment.

- Expecting and enforcing an "honor code" for all members and stakeholders of the organization. Even members of the organization's supply chain should be expected to both honor and ensure the organization's expectations for ethical behavior are supported and respected.

- Taking the necessary corrective action when an ethical transgression has been identified and ensuring everyone knows it, even if it results in a team member's termination.

As you can see, all of the above steps, if implemented in an appropriate fashion, should be capable of establishing and sustaining an ethical corporate culture, and should eventually equate to a well-established and well-known organizational reputation for ethical behavior, corporate citizenship and corporate social responsibility.

"Building the brand" has become quite the buzz phrase for those organizations hoping to instill a high level of dedication and commitment on the part of the employee workforce towards the organization's mission and vision. You should remember Thomas Paine's age-old quote "character is much easier kept than recovered". Well, it is just that simple – your organization builds and sustains a specific reputation just like you do as an individual. Your decisions and actions, or lack thereof, build your own personal and professional reputation. That reputation many times can also be the deciding factor in whether someone does business with your organization or stays with you as a returning customer. Research reveals that customer loyalty is at an all-time low in the United States. Low prices, ease of doing business, incentive packages, and many other variables both inside and outside your control, impact whether an individual client or business continues to do business with you. Any tarnishing of your organization's reputation is likely to impact whether or not you either maintain or gain additional business. Even government entities will tell you the importance reputation can have on your ability to function effectively and ultimately achieve your recognized mission. Just ask the FBI or USMC, and they will explain to you how important your reputation is to your success as an organization. Particularly today, when almost every large organization in the country is having trouble trying to recruit qualified applicants, the role your reputation plays in this process is critical. Many members of the FBI will unequivocally confirm, their reputation as an agency reinforces their success, not only as agents and leaders, but also as an organization. Like the old adage says, "Your reputation precedes you," and every decision you make and every interaction you have with someone either helps build it or destroy it! Good or bad, it certainly does precede you and many times continues following you!

CHAPTER 23

BUILD A HIGH-PERFORMANCE ORGANIZATIONAL CULTURE!

Ensure your individual, team and organizational values support a high-performance culture and positive work environment.

Developing organizational characteristics based upon the core values, guiding principles, ethical standards, policies, processes, standard operating procedures, and best practices in support of the organization's functions and strategic plan, is critical to an organization's success. I believe that the term policy, like bureaucracy, started out as a well-respected and well-meaning term early in the 20th century, but over time, through misuse and abuse, has taken on a negative connotation to the average employee or worker. Whenever there are two or more people working together toward a common goal, there should be agreement by both parties on how they will conduct themselves when the other party is not present. This explains the need for developing and implementing various policies and procedures and how important it is to achieving high performance within any organization today. By developing acceptable practices – "how we do business" – when the organization or its supervisors and leaders are not available to either observe or direct our actions, is one way of creating a positive corporate culture and helping to ensure high performance levels remain intact thus helping to support a strong organizational reputation and brand.

Policy presents the guidelines required of the organization regarding how a specific task, function, initiative, activity, or project within the organization is supposed to be engaged in as part of the employee workforce's regularly expected duties. Procedures, or standard operating procedures (SOPs), are nothing more than the written steps and processes that must be followed when engaging in the above-mentioned activities and policies. It ensures standardization of the methods being utilized in the furtherance of and accomplishment of the organization's mission. If the policies have not been formalized or are not in writing, then there is no standardized method for ensuring that the expectations for completing any identified task or performance objective will be adhered to. When an organization as a whole identifies and agrees to its future direction, the appropriate rules, regulations, policies, and procedures must be developed to support the execution of the many tasks associated with the successful realization of the goals, objectives, and mission of the organization as identified in the strategic plan. Without these same rules, policies, and procedures, both supervisors and workers alike, based upon their own personal feelings, could misinterpret or even intentionally disregard expectations agreed upon by the organization and its top leadership as being acceptable behavior on the part of the organization and its members. Rules, policies, and procedures must be adhered to by both employees and leadership as the organization pushes forward. In order for the organization to maintain its expected productivity, quality control, service levels, running lean, cutting wastes, and risk mitigation activities, we must all learn to follow policy! As stated earlier, one of the greatest threats to organizations today are those that are internal. When team members or even leadership fail to execute their assigned tasks and responsibilities by failing to follow policy or the rules, the organization's "Big 5" measures of success are immediately put in danger. This in turn puts the accomplishment of the organization's mission and vision at risk, which is of course unacceptable!

In a more realistic sense, we must understand that without policies and procedures the organization or its members, due to the legalistic society we live in today, could engage in behavior that puts the organization, its members, or even its stakeholder's performance levels at risk. One of the most critical pieces to ensuring high performance in any organization is identifying, developing, and implementing strong policies and procedures. When an organization has historically engaged in accomplishing its goals and objectives in a very specific manner over a long period of time, informal business practices may begin to become solidified as part of the accepted corporate culture. These informal, yet acceptable ways of "doing business" can be just as powerful a tool in directing the accomplishment of the organization's mission as the formal chain of command and organizational structure. One must never underestimate the power or effect of accepted past business practices and the prevailing and/or past corporate culture. Federal courts have ruled that organizations can be held accountable for these informal ways of doing business, or "the way we do things around here." Therefore, developing the 5 P's (Policy, Procedures, Processes, Practices and Progress) are all critical pieces to helping ensure internal compliance with established statutory and administrative law, or any other official guidelines and rules at hand. Even with the 5 Ps present, it is still absolutely critical that leadership enforce the proper usage of each of the 5 P's, and not allow employees to either modify or ignore these important rules and regulations. Remember, it is impossible as an individual or organization to obtain and sustain high performance levels without following the established rules, policies and work performance standards. These rules and guidelines are all designed to ensure all of the organization's systems and processes work as they were both designed and developed!

CHAPTER 24

BUILD PARTNERSHIPS AND STRATEGIC ALLIANCES, WHILE STAYING TRUE TO YOUR CORE COMPETENCIES!

Remember your Core Competencies, Signature Strengths and Competitive Advantage, and build and sustain both short and long-term relationships.

Building positive relationships is a requirement of success today at all levels, including both "grass roots" up to national levels. No one, whether the smallest governmental entity or largest corporation, can afford to or expect to exist as an island any longer. The world exists in such an arena of interdependence and convergence of efforts, such as outsourcing, globalism, ethnic and cultural diversity, political alliances, free trade, etc., that anyone who cherishes their current viability and success, will undoubtedly continue to both develop and maintain their various relationships in the form of partnerships, alliances, and various other forms of symbiotic relationships. These relationships can be formed intentionally through a well-defined and established public relations team, public information office, community outreach group, or governmental liaison, or formed by more informal alliances and networks, such as an employee simply becoming a member of a specific organization, like a community-based club or professional association. These relationships can become invaluable in the future, should you ever need assistance addressing some type of issue or problem. Positive governmental relations are absolutely critical to many organizations' survival. Please be careful, as this can at times become cumbersome and possibly even an ethics issue, due to the infusion of hidden agendas and lobbying prevalent in many political systems today. Because of the innate cost of political campaigns, many politicians make decisions based upon keeping certain specific individuals or special interest groups happy. With this, they ensure that either an individual's or group's future support and political action committee (PAC) funds remain available to them. Such financial commitments and resources are many times critical to offset the cost of particularly heated or heavily contested political races. Unfortunately, this same phenomenon causes some "elected officials" to unfortunately become career "politicians." Elected officials run for office to represent their constituents, regardless of the political climate or the outcome of their decision to their future viability as an elected official. A career politician, unlike a true elected official, many times allow their decisions to be swayed by the possible outcome of their decision on the future political support they can secure. In short, anyone who has spent time in education, the private sector, government, military, or non-profit sectors, understands the usefulness of developing and maintaining various positive relationships. The key to success in this arena is to take the necessary steps early and support a philosophy of ethical behavior on the part of all employees, the organization and even outside stakeholders.

While we are building such critical relationships and alliances, we must not forget to stick to what we are good at! Stick to your core competencies as an individual and organization. In other words, stick to what you are good at and what works! Keep yourself and the organization focused on the identified mission and agreed upon vision, and don't allow yourself to be swayed into focusing your resources or efforts towards activities that are nice to address in a perfect world, but which do not really make sense for your organization today. Remember, if you start to water down your mission with everything becoming a priority, then nothing is a priority, and you ultimately endanger the success of the entire organization. The United States Coast Guard (USCG) is a perfect example of this phenomenon occurring, where over time and throughout history they have had their organization shift from being called the United States Cutter Service, historically responsible for collecting tariffs on goods being imported or exported within the United States, to the modern USCG, with 11 distinct mission sets they are responsible for. The problem, however, is exasperated even further, because the USCG does not have the necessary resources to successfully accomplish all of their mission sets to the level they desire. In fact, the entire United States Coast Guard have approximately the same number of personnel available for deployment towards these various mission sets as the New York City Police Department has, yet their responsibilities and duties are worldwide!

The U.S.C.G.'s current mission sets include the following:

- Environmental Protection
- Illegal Immigration
- Defense Readiness
- Aids to Navigation
- Port and Waterway Security
- Law Enforcement (Including fight on terrorism)
- Drug Interdiction
- Marine Safety
- Search and Rescue at Sea

TAKE US *to the* TOP

- Ice Operations
- Living Marine Resources

It is quite obvious that a force the size of the USCG with various other worldwide responsibilities cannot possibly hope to carry out so many duties and missions up to the standards that their personnel wish to without securing additional resources. This is just one type of issue that can endanger an organization and its members' morale. Employees can miss the satisfaction from successfully fulfilling the various responsibilities required of their mission and, most importantly, vision. Jim Collins reiterates this same tenet in his book *Good to Great*: *The Social Sectors*, when he states that you must not forget what you are good at – while still remaining vigilant for a possible dynamic capability, should the opportunity present itself. If your organization is always running at or above maximum capacity, with no undedicated time, money, or resources in reserve, then if and when a dynamic opportunity presents itself, you may not have the capacity to adequately and successfully address or take action on it! Always concentrate your resources where your effort will pay the greatest returns, because rarely in this world we live and work in will you ever have all of the resources you would like to have or need to have to effectively execute the many tasks required of your organization's mission. Remain true to your core competencies; identify what you are naturally good at and what you like to do, then go after it with tenacity and the rest will fall into place naturally.

When we speak in America of core competencies and signature strengths, we normally view diversification as always being a positive activity, whether it is your personal investment portfolio, your company's product line, or your employee workforce profile. However, there are times where over-diversification can become a serious issue for the organization. Even Jack Welch, in his now-famous interview with Herb Kelleher of Southwest Airlines, explains that at times he over-diversified General Electric (GE) by purchasing smaller firms and companies, which sometimes resulted in poorer performance, due to GE not really understanding that business' mission or methods thoroughly enough to make good decisions. Even though he was considered the "Godfather" of acquiring other holdings and constantly expanding the GE umbrella as a corporate giant, Welch will be the first to admit that companies should stick to their core competencies and signature strengths first!

Many organizations, operating with limited resources, find themselves having to reinvent the way they do business, just to be able to meet the demands of their primary mission. There are some organizations, however, particularly those in the for-profit sector, which have been fortunate enough to expand their mission and include other diversified entities. As stated, Jack Welch, the former CEO of General Electric (GE), was the first CEO of his time to proactively engage in the practice of planned growth and expansion by purchasing other companies. However, on a smaller scale, there have been many others who believed that quality, not quantity, was the key to success as an organization. For example, Becton, Dickinson and Company of New Jersey, a major provider of high-quality health care products, has long striven for becoming a great, not just good, company. Their former CEO Edward Ludwig envisioned a future organization based upon delivering high quality products and operating a great company with great people. Again, ever since the company's inception in 1897, the emphasis has always been on quality, not size or quantity. You must decide for yourself what your vision and focus will be.

Not everyone can stand to have their missions expanded to a large degree for fear that the limited resources they have at their disposal may not be enough to meet, much less sustain the basic demands of their original mission. This is the specific case for those entities who find themselves as non-profits, educational institutions, or government entities. In the aforementioned types of operating environments, the CEO rarely controls the amount of funding that can be allocated to sustain growth or the expansion of services; therefore, he or she must be very careful not to allow too much diversification or "Mission Creep." "Mission Creep" is defined as the wanted or unwanted expansion of an organization's mission and the commensurate responsibilities that accompany the expanded mission.

With all of this in mind, organizations should focus their resources towards their core competencies and signature strengths. Simply put, core competencies involve an organization concentrating on what it does best. What do we do better than anyone else? What activity or activities is the organization known for, and what fields are we the most competitive in? The competitive advantage that exists for the organization in their area of expertise is where most organizations excel of course. For instance, many large city and state police departments across the country have found themselves thrust into the area of homeland security and anti-terrorism efforts since 9/11. They have recognized that preventing, investigating, and prosecuting various groups' hostile intentions towards the United States, is not solely the responsibility of the federal government. However, with the existing economy across the country, finding the necessary resources to effectively engage in this type of activity can be a real challenge for most police executives, as they continue to try to effectively accomplish all of the duties required of their original mission as a law enforcement agency. There are times however, where the organization may identify an area of concern that requires addressing, with no one else left to shoulder the duties and responsibilities present, they may want to shift a specific number of resources towards the newly identified area. Almost all organizations today operate with limited resources, so it is imperative that top leadership sets a direction toward accomplishing specific, well-identified goals and objectives, and excel at what they should be, even if that means becoming a niche provider of products and services for a very well-defined, specific market. Most anyone or any organization can excel at something given unlimited resources, but the real litmus test comes when you must do many things well, with only the limited number and type of resources provided or available. This type of situation will certainly reveal who can simultaneously remain both efficient and successful!

CHAPTER 25

SUSTAIN SUCCESS THROUGH EFFECTIVE SUCCESSION PLANNING!

Engage in effective Succession Planning to ensure the organization's future viability, by identifying and developing your organization's current and future talent! Team members want a chance to learn, grow and develop themselves both personally and professionally!

In reviewing the requirements of high performance and organizational success, we must remember there are a few key attributes that the organization and its systems must possess.

In list form these characteristics and attributes are:

- Effective corporate governance to provide and help ensure and support the mission, vision, and direction of the organization.
- Great leadership to help drive the vision, direction, and development of the strategic plan.
- A leadership philosophy which fosters and supports organizational high performance.

- A well-qualified, committed, and highly motivated employee workforce and supervisors capable of strategic plan implementation and tasks execution.

- A systems approach, capable of harnessing and directing all of the processes and efforts required of today's organizations.

- Accountability built into and embedded throughout the organization as part of the corporate culture via continually measuring individual, team, and organizational performance.

Remember! Adding value is the reason behind every action completed within the organization. If every action or behavior taken within the organization is designed for and results in increased value for the organization, then you are effectively solidifying the organization's future position as a leader in its designated field. Succession planning, the long-term planning and preparation required of a seamless transition from one organizational leader to another, has long been considered important, yet in reality it does not receive much more than lip service in many organizations. There appears to be two very different philosophies on succession planning: one, that it is not only important, but critical to the current and future viability of the organization, ensuring operations will not be adversely impacted by a transition in middle management or top leadership; or two, that a true succession plan is not really necessary and that the organization has survived these changes in leadership before, and so they will in fact surely survive again, without ever formally recognizing or preparing for the change itself.

In many organizations, there is no apparent need for succession planning, because historically the organization's governing entity has always decided to "go outside" when identifying a new top leadership team for the organization. Large corporations, hospitals, school districts, and even many churches are notorious for this type of leadership transition. However, there are others who do not believe this is the most efficient method of transitioning to new leadership. The United States military, most police and fire departments, small businesses, large progressive and well-run companies, and most startups and entrepreneurial ventures find it more beneficial to identify possible future key players and leaders from within the organization, and to start developing their skill sets and abilities early, all in an effort to seamlessly transition them into top leadership positions as they are needed. Lateral entry is the key term to remember when determining whether an organization needs to engage in effective succession planning. Lateral entry is the selection and hiring of a person from an outside entity and positioning them in your organization at a comparable or higher rank or position than they hold in their current organization.

Before we discuss lateral entry and its effect on succession planning, we must first study some of the more obvious positive and negative effects lateral entry has on an organization: Possible advantages of lateral entry are as follows:

- When needed and at will, the organization can post any position and instantaneously engage in a regional, national, or international search for new middle management or top leadership.
- The organization can attempt to steal another organization's very best, including their skills, knowledge, ability, vision, work ethic, reputation etc.
- The organization does not have to identify early on what skillsets or types of personality traits they might be looking for in their top leadership.
- It allows organizational governance to bring in a "reformist" to modify past poor practices or performance and to "change the direction" of the organization.

- Due to the person coming in, they can impact the organization more quickly by having what is either a real or perceived more diverse background, work experiences, or past successes.

- Top organizational governance can also identify someone from the outside who has past successes under their belt and who has proven what they can accomplish.

- An outsider is more likely to "whip the organization into shape", because of their lack of interpersonal relationships with other members of the organization; they will "not be leading their friends," which in many organizations causes a whole litany of other problems, issues and concerns.

- When promoting someone up from inside the organization you are not always sure what you are going to get. There is the "Peter Principle" where people get promoted up to their final level of incompetence.

- It allows the organization to not expend valuable time and resources on engaging in future planning efforts, including the training and education required of developing current talent.

Possible disadvantages of lateral entry use are:

- All employees are only moderately motivated to work because they realize, due to the past history of the organization, that they have no chance at being selected to move up to the "top spot".

- Motivation to work harder or smarter, or to strive for high performance, wanes because it is an accepted practice and part of the company culture that no matter how hard you work or how qualified you are, new leadership comes from the outside.

- Morale and motivation to work hard or perform highly is stymied, which consistently causes lower productivity, quality control, and even ethical issues to arise. The old adage "if you want good behavior or performance to be repeated, you must reward it" does not necessarily hold true.

- Going outside can many times cost more directly and indirectly via the intensive and sometimes exhaustive search process.

- You are never quite sure how the new leadership team will perform in the new environment thus increasing the risk of the unknown.

- The salary and benefits packages are almost always inflated in an effort on the part of the new leader to protect themselves should they not do well or be asked to leave prematurely.

- Many times, organizational governance is willing to authorize an inflated salary and benefits package during the search effort, in the hope they can attract someone with all the many attributes and qualifications they are looking for.

We should be aware that there are professional CEOs who move around constantly and yet have never shown a vested interest in how things go within the organization currently employing them, except to keep building their own personal and professional résumé, in an effort to command more money for the next job or position they compete for. Subsequently, the new person does not have any historical perspective on the problems, issues, or concerns faced by the organization, and hence he or she is also not privy to all of the many "skeletons hiding in closets", or the "land mines" that might be waiting for them within the organization as they proceed.

Lateral entry allows a great deal of internal and external politics to be played by the newly selected CEO, such as "pulling strings" and lining up "sweetheart" deals for those who they know or owe, and even by bringing other outsiders onboard and placing them in jobs they may not necessarily be well-suited for or even meet the position's minimum qualifications. Also, the new leader may not completely understand the past and current organizational culture and subcultures, and so when reorganizing, they do not necessarily know what the past serious issues are and where they are and can therefore commit CEO "career suicide" by being ignorant of the current or past organizational environment or climate.

As one can see, the topic of whether to engage in a successful succession planning program is based in great part on the organizational governance's philosophy towards top leadership. If an organization is not performing well, then the prevailing perception might exist that someone must be brought in from the outside, because only an outsider can correct the negative effect that having someone promoted from within did to the organization last time. There are no easy answers. As an outside consultant, however, with no vested interest in my answer to this question, I would posit that there are times when lateral entry is indeed required. However, I also believe every organization should possess, if possible, well-designed and agreed upon career development and employee growth programs, that ultimately result in an effective succession plan being in place, thus allowing for a seamless "changing of the guard" when the time comes. This will equate to less stress, fewer costs, and a more highly motivated workforce throughout the organization, particularly if implemented correctly!

CONCLUSION

Will you lead your organization to success? I believe we have successfully established that leadership sets, drives, and sustains an organization's corporate culture, whether good or bad. From setting direction, to establishing core values, developing a positive reputation and brand, to building positive traditions through continuing to demand that the established work performance standards be adhered to, leadership does in fact drive corporate culture. We must remember that top leadership not only sets the direction for everyone, but also devises the plan on how everyone is going to get there. Even the organization's strategic plan has to establish and support a positive corporate culture in order to enforce all of the core values the organization subscribes to. Leadership should build and sustain a corporate culture that thrives on high performance and success at every level. Know yourself, know your followers, know your organization, and stick to what you are good at. Using Situational/Contingent leadership, fused with effective Servant leadership is critical to both leadership and organizational success. Team members can spot a phony a mile away. Be yourself and work hard every day at being a great leader, then drive yourself, your team, your business unit, and the entire organization towards high performance and success!

In conclusion, experience and research both suggest that leadership and effective supervisory management practices are required at every level of the organization if it is to achieve high performance and success! Too many times it is not only entry-level employees who blame top leadership for the ills of the organization, but first line supervisors and mid-level managers blame top leadership too. When a person agrees to accept the remuneration, power, and privileges which come with a promotion to supervise, manage, or lead, they must also be willing to accept the additional duties, responsibilities and accountability which come with the job, one of which is now being "neither fish nor fowl." This newfound leadership position may have long been what you had hoped for and wished for; however, as the old adage states, "careful what you wish for, it might come true." Now you are no longer just an employee – one of the "masses" – but you must now have an additional allegiance and understanding about the effective and successful administration of the organization. Your job is to not only ensure everyone works harder and smarter, but to ensure that everyone for whom you supervise and are responsible for is giving their best effort and living up to their full potential while at work. As stated earlier and reiterated throughout, for an organization to reach those high levels of performance, leadership must find itself working effectively at every level, position, and entity which comprise today's complex organizations. From operations to administration and even support services, all organizations today, whether large or small, need to find a way to foster high performance. This is all in an effort to accomplish their identified mission and vision in an exemplary fashion. Leadership drives this success, and although finding the magic formula for leading an organization successfully can sometimes be an elusive goal, it is one we should accept the challenge of and strive towards, if we ever hope to excel in such a competitive world.

The critical steps to both leadership and organizational success:

- Study your organization thoroughly, including its mission, vision, administration, operations and supports services duties and responsibilities.
- Gain input and buy in and sell your shared vision to all stakeholders.
- Set direction and develop a strategic plan.
- Resource the plan, from identifying the funding required to effectively recruit and manage the talent available to securing the necessary technology needed.
- Implement the plan and continually manage the processes and systems functionality.
- Assess progress and make necessary or desired adjustments where required.
- Always remain alert to the changing tides of the world you work in and remain vigilant of any possible dynamic opportunities that may present themselves.

Follow these steps and remain committed to individual, team, division, and organizational success! Never become satisfied with the status quo and your past successes, and follow the guidance provided here, and you will surely be on your way to becoming a great leader in a successful organization! Remember you are only as good as your last performance!!!!!

Just remember, in the end it comes down to this –

"Do you have the courage to be a great leader?"
and
*"Does your organization have the will
to let you be one?"*

REFERENCES

Arredondo, L. (2000). *Communicating Effectively.* Madison, WI: CWL Publishing Enterprises.

Blanchard, K., & Johnson, S. (1983). *The One Minute Manager.* New York, NY: Berkley Books.

Certo, S. C. (2008). *Supervision, Concepts & Skill-Building* (6th ed.). New York, NY: McGraw-Hill/Irwin.

Collins, J. (2001). Good to Great. Jim Collins. New York, NY: Harper-Collins

Collins, J. (2005). *Good to Great and the Social Sectors.* Jim Collins. New York, NY: Harper-Collins.

Covey, S. R. (1989). *The 7 Habits of Highly Effective People.* New York, NY: Simon & Schuster.

Dale, Nancy "Turning Around an Organization: How the Fort Pierce Police Department Did It,"

Law and Order[end] 48 (November 2000): 87–91.

DeKluyver, C. A., & Pearce II, J. A. (2006). *Strategy, A View from the Top.* Upper Saddle RIver, NJ: Pearson Education, Inc.

Fortune. (2011, December 12). Howard Schultz. *Fortune,* pp. 105-115.

Fournies, F. F. (2007). *Why Employees Don't Do What They're Supposed to Do.* New York, NY: McGraw-Hill.

Frank, M. S. (n.d.). The History of American Management Thought: A Perspective and Analysis.

Fritz, R. (2001). *Think Life A Manager* (3rd ed.). Franklin Lakes, NJ: Career Press.

Gaither, N., & Frazier, G. (2002). *Operations Management* (9th ed.). Mason, OH: South-Western.

Hammer, M. (2001). *The Agenda.* New York, NY: Crown Business.

Henry, Vincent the CompStat Paradigm: Management Accountability in Policing, Business, and the Public Sector Lushing, N.Y.: Looseleaf Law Pub 2002, 1–3.

Houston Police Department, "Two HPD Divisions Receive Prestigious Certification," news release, October 12, 2011,

Howe, N., & Strauss, W. (2007). *Millenials Go to College* (2nd ed.). LifeCourse Associates.

Hynes, G. E. (2008). *Managerial Communication* (4th ed.). New York, NY: McGraw-Hill/Irwin.

Indeed.com Editorial Team, March 2023, USDecipher/FocusVision.

Maxwell, J. C. (1999). *The 21 Indispensable Qualities of a Leader.* Nashville, TN: Thomas Nelson, Inc.

Natemeyer, W. E., & Hersey, P. (2011). *Classics of Organizational Behavior* (4th ed.). Long Grove, IL: Waveland Press.

Northouse, P. G. (2010). *Leadership.* Thousand Oaks, CA: SAGE Publications, Inc.

Perkins, T. (2007). *Valley Boy* (1st ed.). New York, NY: Gotham Books.

Pfeffer, J. (2016, January). Getting Beyond the BS of Leadership LIterature. *McKinsey Quarterly*, pp. 1-5.

Philpot, T. (2008, June). Mission to Organize. *Military Officer*, pp. 55-59, 79, 85, 87, 91.

Jerry H. Ratcliffe and Ray Guidetti, "State Police Investigative Structure and the Adoption of

Intelligence-Led Policing," Policing: An International Journal of Police Strategies and Management, 31, no. 1 (2008): 109–128

Riggio, R. E. (2003). *Industrial/Organizational Psychology* (4th ed.). Upper Saddle River: Prentice Hall.

Senge, P. M. (2006). *The Fifth Discipline*. New York, NY: Doubleday.

Shapiro, R. M., & Jordan, G. (2008). *Dare to Prepare*. New York, NY: Crown Business.

The Drucker Foundation. (2001). *A Conversation with Peter F. Drucker & Peter M. Sence*. New York, NY: Jossey-Bass.

Wagner III, J. A., & Hollenbeck, J. R. (1995). *Management of Organizational Behavior* (2nd ed.). Englewood Cliffs, NJ: Prentice Hall.

Warren, G.A. "The Warren Integrated Strategic Management System" model, Police Chief, March 2012

Wilmington, DE. Strategic Management Research Center, 2010).

Welch, J., & Byrne, J. A. (2001). *Jack*. New York, NY: Warner Books.

Wendover, R. W. (2007). *Smart Hiring*. Naperville, IL: Sourcebooks, Inc.

INDEX

ABOUT THE AUTHOR

Dr. Gregory Warren is a twenty-two-year veteran of the Delaware State Police, retiring in 2005, as the Director of Training for the Division of State Police in Delaware. During his career, he served as a uniform trooper, patrol commander, Director of Community Services, Director of Planning, and Troop Commander. Dr. Warren also served as the Administrator for the Delaware Council on Police Training. He retired again in 2021 after 13 years as a professor and the program chair, for the Masters in the Administration of Justice and Masters in Homeland Security programs at Wilmington University.

Dr. Warren has written numerous articles on leadership development and organizational performance. He focuses much of his writing, teaching and consulting on the criticality of individual, team and leadership performance to organizational success. His new leadership development and performance management program focuses on providing comprehensive situational performance and decision-based organizational leadership training to all members of organizations, regardless of position, rank or seniority.

Dr. Warren also presents on a variety of subjects critical to effective public safety operations today, ranging from Successful Strategic Planning, to Advanced LE Ethics, Conflict Management and De-escalation Techniques, Risk Prevention and Mitigation and the Situational Policing model. He is a certified master instructor and has trained tens of thousands of public safety personnel.

Dr. Warren holds his Doctorate Degree in Vocational Education from Temple University. He also holds an associate degree in police science, a bachelor's degree in criminal justice, a bachelor's degree in behavioral science, a master's degree in supervisory management, and is a graduate of Northwestern University's School of Police Staff and Command.

For information about his services or speaking opportunities, please visit American Law Enforcement Training and Consulting at https:// americanletc.com/.